THE

CRUMBLING

OF A

NATION

AND OTHER STORIES

RYAN DAVID GINSBERG

The stories *Tommy Longhorn*, *Amber's Son*, *A Million Times Over Again*, *The Termination Bureau*, *A Baby is Born*, *The Unknown Writer*, and *Dinner and a Show* first appeared in *It Was Just Another Day in America: a collection of poems and stories*, though they have since been revised.

The last story, *In the Algorithm We Trust*, contains the first three chapters of a work in progress of the same name. If you are an agent or publisher interested in reading the entire manuscript, hit me up.

Hardcover and eBook cover design by Christian Storm
Paperback cover design by Barış Şehri

TikTok Special Edition: 9781980783770
Hardcover: 9798986976679
Paperback: 9798986976648
eBook: 9798986976655

The Ginsberg Publishing House

TO

QUINTON

TABLE OF CONTENTS

Tommy

Longhorn

APPROACHING THE MILKY WAY GALAXY at a speed once thought to be impossible is a ship captained by an extraterrestrial being whose name is best translated into the English language as Tommy Longhorn, and a telescope manned by the highest-ranking squadron in the US Space Force is aimed directly at it.

It is the sighting these soldiers have waited their entire careers for:

A real-life UFO.

The telescope they are looking through is attached to a high-powered Astroblaster created to shoot down any extraterrestrial threat to their nation of birth—the United States of America.

However, the soldiers do not shoot, nor do they even flinch at the sight of the ship, for they are unable to see it for what it truly is. You see, Tommy Longhorn, the extraterrestrial captain of the ship, has turned the exterior camouflage setting to the 'ON' position. As a result, the soldiers see in the ship's place just a tiny speck of space dust—though that speck does not remain in their vision for long.

"Rotate!" commands the general, and so the soldiers angle their Astroblaster a single degree to the right, a procedure that takes the entire squadron and several minutes to accomplish.

And with that tiny movement, the speck of space dust that is, in actuality, an extraterrestrial ship nearly three square miles in size vanishes from sight.

"Oorah," says the general.

"Oorah," say the soldiers in unison.

And together the squadron studies every inch of the new piece of space now visible to them for any potential threat to the United States of America—though all they see is space dust.

Tommy Longhorn is a member of a universe-wide coalition of species known as the Confederation of the Cosmos. The Confederation has been in existence for billions of years. It consists of tens of billions of species from tens of billions of planets located throughout hundreds of millions of galaxies. The Confederation is constantly searching the Universe for more species to add to this already large coalition, resulting in a never-ending exploration of the Universe, of which Tommy Longhorn has become an integral part.

He is a Planet Explorer.

His duty is to travel to planets upon which intelligent lifeforms have been discovered and live among the species. He integrates with their society, observes their way of life—their culture, their beliefs, their actions. He enters into relationships with members of that species, eats their foods, worships their gods, reads their literature, observes their art, studies their architecture, learns their laws, practices their politics, plays their games, attends their schools, participates in their...

He lives life as it is lived on the assigned planet, for that is the only way to truly understand a species.

After completing his observations of said planet, he is tasked with the responsibility of recommending to the Governmental Board of the Confederation whether or not the studied species should receive an invitation to join the Confederation.

And so it came to be that Tommy Longhorn, an extraterrestrial being, a member of the Confederation of the Cosmos, and a Planet Explorer, found himself on a ship disguised as a speck of space dust located many, many lightyears away from his home planet, bound for the Milky Way Galaxy:

More specifically, bound for the planet Earth.

In his office, he prepares for arrival.

This office is filled with hundreds of thousands of books written in thousands of languages from thousands of species from all across the Universe, all of which he can read with ease despite being monolingual, thanks to his Omni-Lingual Lenses, which, when turned to the proper setting, translate every written word in front of him to his native tongue of Klementyme. Among the books, sitting randomly upon the shelves, are little knick-knacks to remind him of home: a necklace his mother used to wear, an old uniform of his father's, some pictures drawn by his kids, and various figurines, among other things.

Hanging on the wall across from his desk is a picture, a painting, and a piece of paper, all in matching frames.

The picture shows Tommy, his wife, and his four children taken the day before his departure. Tommy is quite large, even for his species, standing at just under ten feet and weighing just north of 800 pounds. He has thick, blubbery skin, like that of a hippopotamus. That skin is a bright purple, nearly luminous. He has four arms and four legs. He has six eyes, all of which blink entirely out of sync, with no two ever closing simultaneously and with no obvious rhyme or reason to the order in which they blink. One eye may blink four, five, six times before another blinks at all. As for his wife, she is pale green. Her skin is anything but luminous. She is much shorter than Tommy, standing at roughly seven and a half feet and weighing roughly 500 pounds. As for their children, one son and three daughters, they are all varying shades of blue—some light, some dark—and stand at roughly eight feet, give or take a couple of inches.

To the left of this family portrait is the letter Tommy Longhorn and his mother received when he was a child, announcing the death of his father, who was, like Tommy is now, a Planet Explorer. His father had completed sixteen missions before the one that finally killed him. After all communication had been lost between the Planet Exploration Group and his father, a team of Galaxy Defenders was sent to the planet his father was exploring, existing somewhere in the Andromeda Galaxy. Upon investigation, the Galaxy Defenders discovered that his father's identity as an extraterrestrial being had been detected by the species of this foreign planet and that he had been hanged in the square of the planet's capital. His body, which had already begun to rot, was still hanging in the square when the Galaxy Defenders discovered it, along with a sign upon which had been written words that were too gruesome to be copied in the letter. In the middle of the night, the Galaxy Defenders cut down his father's body, brought it to their ship, and flew it back to his home planet, where he was given a proper and honorable burial.

The letter was signed by the highest-ranking members of the Planet Exploration Group, along with small, personal messages of grief and sorrow.

And no, the species that killed his father did not receive an invitation to the Confederation of the Cosmos. Instead, they were placed on a list of species considered to be severe threats to the Universe itself.

They have been kept under close watch ever since.

To the right of the family portrait is a painting of the entrance to the Planet Collective on the day it first opened to the public. Tommy has always been obsessed with the Planet Collective. He visited many times as a child and takes his own kids to visit every time he has the chance, his most recent visit being just two months ago.

The Planet Collective is a scientific haven involving a synthetic solar system built around a sun long ago discovered to have an empty orbit. It was an idea thought up by a group of the Confederation's most prestigious scientists, where they bring in small groups of every species discovered in the Known Universe to live in the Planet Collective, allowing scientists from all over to perform all sorts of experiments with all sorts of species while never needing to leave this singular solar system.

Over a span of multiple millennia, this collective of scientists, whose members are constantly changing as the generations come and go, have created thousands of planets of various sizes and distances for that once lonely sun. On each planet, they have constructed thousands of habitats that emulate those found throughout the Universe. And as more species are discovered each day, the quicker the Planet Collective continues to expand.

A synthetic planet is currently being constructed to emulate that of the planet Earth, upon which scientists hope to carry out experiments for billions of years to come—experiments that can help the Confederation understand even more than they already do about life, evolution, and intelligence.

But before any studies can take place in the Planet Collective involving the species of planet Earth, Tommy Longhorn must first complete his observations.

And so, as he sits in his office—in front of a picture, a painting, and a letter—he prepares for those observations by studying the 12,093-page portfolio prepared for him by the thousands of Life Inspectors who visited the planet Earth before it was decided that the planet, and more importantly its apex creature, was finally ready for a Planet Explorer like Tommy Longhorn to conduct a more thorough exploration, evaluation, and recommendation.

In this portfolio, hundreds of millions of years' worth of research, observations, and experimentations have been summarized for Tommy Longhorn, including the geographical breakdown of the Earth, the chemical makeup of its atmosphere, the strength of its gravity, and so much more.

But most important of all, the portfolio provides him with the information he needs to best understand the planet's apex creature: the species he has been sent to the planet Earth to study, the species that will one day be added to the Planet Collective, the species he will soon live among:

Human beings.

The first 500 pages are filled with sketches of human beings, providing the chronological evolution of the species, physically and societally, over a duration of nearly four million years. The next 1,000 pages are filled with photographs, handwritten notes, laboratory experiments, x-ray scans, copies of memos sent to and received from the Planet Exploration Group, transcripts of conversations had with various human beings, letters written to 'the Planet Explorer eventually assigned to the planet Earth', and so much more.

The final 8,000 pages discuss the over 4,000 human beings the final Life Inspector abducted during her final 783 visits to the planet, upon whom incredibly invasive experiments were conducted, externally and internally.

As a result of these experiments, three critical technologies were created to aid Tommy Longhorn in his observations of the planet.

The first is a bodysuit that will allow him to camouflage himself as a human being with just the push of a button. The second is a speaking device that will translate any word spoken by Tommy Longhorn from his native tongue of Klementyme into a language the human being he is talking to can understand. And the third is a hearing device that works in the exact opposite manner, translating their words into Klementyme.

For the only way Tommy Longhorn can understand what it is like to be a human being is to *be* a human being—or at least to be as close to a human being as is scientifically possible for him to be.

While still a few hours away from Earth, he puts the portfolio down and goes to the kitchen. He grabs a tray of food from the icebox and places it in a machine similar in appearance to that of a microwave on Earth, only it does not have any buttons and certainly does not operate like a microwave. Once the door to the machine has closed, the food inside is scanned and the ideal temperature of each item is determined.

After a few moments, the device dings gently, softly.

He opens the door and grabs the tray and takes it to the table across the way and sits down to eat. On the tray is a thick piece of what looks like T-bone steak, only the meat is dark grey and the fat is light yellow and the bone is neon green and the meat is not actually meat at all. Next to it is a pinkish blob of mashed-up fruit topped with an incredibly thick blue gravy. Scattering the tray, taking up the spaces in between, is a medley of vegetables that look nearly identical to a Peppermint Swirl, though they are soft and crumble in the mouth.

He does not use any silverware to eat this meal. He simply grabs the ice-cold T-bone steak-looking thing, tears off a small piece with ease, dips it into the smashed fruit and blue gravy, which is scalding hot, and stuffs it in his mouth. He then chases it down with a multicolored liquid—so thick it almost needs to be chewed—which tastes nearly identical to a cup of dark roast coffee served with light cream and two packets of Splenda.

Soon, Pluto is passing him by. Then Neptune. Then Uranus. Then Saturn. Then Jupiter. Then Mars.

An alarm begins to sound—DIIIIIIIIIIIIIIIIIIIIIIIIIIIIIIIING! DIIIIIIIIIIIIIIIIIIIIIIIIIIIIIIIING! DIIIIIIIIIIIIIIIIIIIIIIIIIIIIIIIING! —indicating the ship is approaching the atmosphere of Earth.

Hearing this, he makes his way to the control panel at the front of the ship. With the push of a button, the yank of a pulley, and the sliding of a few fingers across a screen, he adjusts the exterior appearance of his ship, transforming it from a piece of space dust into a common flying species of Earth.

As the ship, which now looks like a seagull, continues its descent, he slides his blubbery, purple skin into an all-black bodysuit, first by putting his four legs into their proper slots and then by doing the same with his four arms. After squeezing his large stomach into the suit, he slides the mask over his head and zips it around his neck.

There is a small band wrapped around one of his wrists that looks almost like a wristwatch. He pushes a few buttons and scrolls until he finds the proper setting that allows him to transform his body into the shape of the Earth's most dominant species:

Human being.

With the final push of a button, his body begins to transform, one part at a time. His four arms turn into two, as do his legs. Four of his eyes are swallowed into his face while the remaining two slide into their new spots and shrink to the proper size. And as uncomfortable as it is for him, those two eyes begin to blink in perfect synchrony, providing him with, for the first time in his life, brief moments of temporary blindness. His two remaining arms recoil and shrink in mass, and his two legs do the same. His head shrinks and deforms out of a perfect sphere. His neck loses flexibility. His purple, blubbery skin becomes tan and hairy, rough and oily.

And, just like that, he is a human being.

At least in appearance.

As the ship lands on a little strip of beach located just a few miles away from the US Space Force base, Tommy Longhorn, now very human in appearance, finishes his final chores. He takes some books and places them back on their proper shelves. He cleans the dishes, reseals some bags of food, takes a few vitamins, and tests the tightness of lids containing chemicals that are poisonous to the planet Earth and its species, yet chemicals he relies on for life. He double-checks every strap, ensures every machine is turned off, and locks every door and cabinet within the ship.

Finished with his work, he says aloud, "My name is Tommy

Longhorn. I am a Planet Explorer from the Confederation of the Cosmos. I am here to observe your apex species, which you call human beings." He speaks these words in his native tongue, but the mouthpiece translates them into the language of Portuguese, which sounds to him like complete gibberish—totally alien. He then takes the earpiece, puts it in his left ear, and repeats the phrase. "My name is Tommy Longhorn. I am a Planet Explorer from the Confederation of the Cosmos. I am here to observe your apex species, which you call human beings." This time, he hears the words in Klementyme, perfectly translated back to him.

Satisfied with the results, he exits the ship.

If anyone had been observing, they would have seen a full-sized human being exiting through the mouth of an open-beaked seagull. However, nobody is near enough to see it, for the nearest human beings are all circled around a telescope attached to an Astroblaster aimed at the stars, allowing for the sight of a human being exiting the mouth of a seagull to go entirely unnoticed.

Tommy Longhorn grabs the seagull and holds it in his human-looking hand. He lifts the seagull's left wing and pokes at its side, at a little keypad. After entering the proper combination, the seagull transforms into a green marble that Tommy places in his bodysuit pocket, which appears to the outside world like a pair of distressed denim jeans.

All of this occurs seamlessly—the transformation of an alien ship into a little green marble and an 800-pound extraterrestrial being into a 263-pound human being and an all-black bodysuit into a graphic T-shirt and distressed jeans—because of a discovery made billions of years ago by a team of scientists in the field of relativity.

The ship is still a ship, Tommy Longhorn is still an 800-pound extraterrestrial being, and the bodysuit is still a bodysuit, only they appear to be something else relative to the things around them.

The technological advantages of this particular discovery can be seen all over the Confederation, where billions of beings the size of Tommy Longhorn live in booming cities the size of a single city block on the planet Earth. Houses appear on the outside to be the size of a single mint, but once inside, they are large enough to make the most elite human being green with envy. And the same goes for the rest of the buildings in their cities: the restaurants, the stores, the office buildings, the towers. The vehicles are all the size of an ant. The streets are just a few inches in width. Parks are the size of a single fallen leaf.

And so on.

But all that is now tens of thousands of lightyears away as Tommy Longhorn walks the long, empty strip of an Earthly beach located just a few miles away from the soldiers who continue to search the cosmos for something—anything!—that may threaten their great nation.

"Oorah!" says the general.

"Oorah!" say the soldiers.

Tommy Longhorn does not come across a single human being as he walks along the beach. Though he does find a couple of crabs and some sand dollars and many piles of trash and some seaweed and several other species and items that are of no interest to him or the Confederation. So he enters the forest near the beach, where he finds bugs crawling through the dirt, squirrels sputtering through the trees, and birds flying through the sky overhead.

And while he appears to the outside world as just another human, he is still very much an extraterrestrial being, one with tendencies and abilities never before seen in a human. So, as he walks deeper into the forest, it does not feel strange for him to get down on his hands and knees so that he can better sniff the ground as he crawls from location to location. It also feels entirely natural to drop his right ear to the ground and listen for several minutes to the sounds of the Earth itself. He listens to vibrations miles away. He pinpoints the location of roots beneath him, as well as crawling insects, and uses the information to map an escape from the forest.

After determining that the exit of the forest is located quite a distance away, too far for his mind to yet see, he presses his palms, which are human only in appearance, into the mud.

He lies flat on the ground.

He breathes in slowly, then out even more slower.

The depth of his vision expands drastically, until—

He suddenly stands and sprints eastward through the forest. His sprint speed is not only quicker than any human being on the planet but is quicker than *any* being on the planet. His strides are unnaturally long relative to the human body he presents to the world, so that it looks as if he is long jumping with each step he takes.

As he runs, he continues to gain speed, his strides growing longer with each step. He leaps over tree limbs, breaks apart herds of deer, chases away flocks of birds, skips over flowing rivers, climbs over mountains on all four, then soars over little hills with arms-a-flapping...

He emerges from the forest, where he finds himself on the edge of a human city.

And, as if he has not just been running at nearly two hundred miles per hour, he comes to an immediate stop.

He stands there for quite some time, in the place where the forest meets the city, looking out at hundreds of human beings.

All of whom look just like him.

Or rather, he looks like them.

After a moment, he enters the city.

At first, he studies not the people, but the city itself. He looks at the buildings. He presses his hands against them and feels their sturdiness. He studies the architectural choices, as well as engineering. He does this for quite some time, walking from block to block, carefully studying all types of buildings—large and small.

He finds an empty bench and sits and watches as the cars drive by, as the birds soar through the sky, as the lights turn from green to yellow to red.

He inhales the scent of Earth, holds it in his nose for as long he can, then exhales the scent gently back to where it belongs.

After a short while, he is up again, walking the streets of this Earthly city.

Though now his eyes are no longer on the buildings.

Instead, they are on the human beings.

Over the next few years, Tommy Longhorn does everything possible to experience life as a human being would experience it. He frequently changes the settings of his bodysuit to present himself as all types of humans—young and old, male and female, fat and skinny, tall and short, white and brown, hairy and smooth, muscular and otherwise.

He avoids none.

He embraces all.

He sits among the congregations at various churches, mosques, synagogues, and temples. He meets with religious leaders, reads sacred texts, and visits holy sites. He sits in classrooms of differing levels all around the world and studies humanity's understanding of mathematics, science, and written language. He attends music festivals and firework shows and soccer games and amusement parks. He visits the Pyramids of Giza, the statues on Easter Island, the Great Wall of China, the Taj Mahal, and the concentration camps scattered around Eastern Europe. He reads their most popular literature, attends the museums that contain their most famous artworks, and watches the movies they have deemed to be award-worthy. He visits large cities and small towns and desolate villages and shantytowns. He listens to political debates among all types of people, across all lands, but never interjects with his beliefs. He learns about the internet and explores every aspect of it. He sits with the down-and-out and feasts with the elite. He studies the effects of humankind's presence on the Earth itself. He takes dozens of human beings back to his ship, which he disguises as a human home, and engages in sexual relations for the benefit of scientific discovery. He celebrates their holidays. He visits their zoos.

And at the end of each day, he removes the green marble from his pocket, sets it on the ground, and walks inside. He adjusts the settings on his wristband and transforms back to his natural self— all ten feet of him. He removes the bodysuit and sets it back in the closet. He goes into his office and sits behind his desk. He looks up at the picture, the painting, and the letter. He remembers his mission, his goal, his reasons for being there.

Then he opens his notebook and writes of his latest discoveries.

And when he is done, he sends those daily notes to the Planet Exploration Group for storage.

He continues these explorations for nearly a decade. Exploring every inch of the planet. Every country, every culture, every people.

And then, on his final night on Earth, as he has done every night before it, he calls his wife using his Telecommunication Cube— though this time it is to tell her that he is finally coming home. As this grey, sleek box sends its signals to his wife's Telecommunication Cube, located tens of thousands of lightyears away, he sets it on the desk and preoccupies himself with various chores. He makes himself dinner. He cleans up the ship. He does some laundry. He reads a few pages from an Earth novel called *The Hitchhiker's Guide to the Galaxy* and giggles at humanity's view of extraterrestrial life and society.

After nearly two hours, there is a dinging sound, indicating the connection has been made. He returns to his office and stands a few feet in front of the Cube. It takes another minute or so for his wife to appear. When she does, a jet of green light shoots out of the Cube, forming her shape above it—all seven and a half feet of her squeezed into just a couple of inches.

"My love," she says, "how is the planet Earth doing today?"

"It is snowing outside," says Tommy in response. "But that is not why I have called you. My dear, I have some wonderful news."

He explains to her that he will be leaving in the morning. That he is just one night's rest away from returning home to her and the kids.

"I will be in your arms soon, my love. Very soon," he says. "I am going to buy you and the kids some final souvenirs. I cannot wait to see you. I cannot wait to see the kids. Send them my love, my dear. Tell them Daddy will see them soon."

With the ship in his pocket, disguised again as a marble, Tommy Longhorn enters a grand shopping mall. One of those shopping malls with multiple stories. The type of mall that extends for multiple blocks and requires a bridge to move from one building to the next. The kind of mall with two food courts and several fine dining options—not *real* fine dining, but the sort of dining that is fine when inside of a mall.

The mall is filled to the brim with human beings shopping for last-minute gifts. Decorated trees can be seen in every window, along with cotton designed to mimic the snow outside. In the mall's center is an old-looking human being, male, with a long white beard. He is wearing a red suit and sits on a throne-like chair. A line of children wait their turn to sit on his lap, a tradition Tommy Longhorn has seen take place annually during his time on the planet Earth, a tradition he has even partaken in—as both bearded man and young child on lap.

However, on this occasion, no longer looking to explore, wanting only to shop, he walks past the bearded man, past the line of kids, past the parents, past the photographer, and into the nearest store.

He picks out a couple of items and takes them to the register.

"$354.21," says the cashier.

Tommy takes a couple of rocks from his pocket and sets them down on the counter, though thanks to the science of relativity, the rocks now look like the $354.21 he owes. The cashier grabs the rocks and feels no difference between them and the money he has seen and felt all his life. He puts the rocks in the register, grabs the receipt, places it in the bag, and hands it to Tommy.

"Merry Christmas," he says.

"Merry Christmas," Tommy says.

The next store has a bunch of figurines, posters, framed photographs, games, and so on. Tommy picks a few games out for him and his family to play when he gets home.

This time he pays for the items with some pocket lint.

As he makes his way to the next store, he notices a few human beings running in his direction. And then dozens more. There is panic on each of their faces, tears streaming down their cheeks. The holiday cheer has suddenly been stripped from the mall.

Nobody says a word, yet everyone knows exactly what to do and where to go.

Like they have rehearsed this all before.

The throne is now empty. The line is gone. The photographers have vanished.

They have all become a blur, a mass of panicked runners, screamers, and sounds Tommy Longhorn does not recognize.

Before he can determine what is happening, a bullet enters what appears to be his stomach, but is actually his heart. He drops to the floor—the presents for his family spill out of their bags.

Purple blood flows from the bullet hole.

From his pocket rolls a little green marble. It rolls and it rolls and it rolls, until a child running away from the shooter slips on the marble and falls to the ground.

The shooter stands over the kid, and shoots.

The red blood of the child mixes with the purple blood of Tommy Longhorn.

A few miles away, soldiers for the US Space Force crowd around an

Astroblaster. They stare at an empty piece of space, at nothing more than space dust, searching for the next threat to their great nation.

"Oorah," says the general.

"Oorah," say the soldiers.

Every night for the next few weeks, Tommy Longhorn's son climbs to the roof of their home and studies the sky above the space station across town as he waits for his father to come home.

Each time a spaceship approaches, he grabs his glasses, places them over his eyes, and adjusts the settings until he can see far enough in the distance for the words on the side of the ship to become clear and legible.

And each time he is disappointed to discover the ship approaching is not his father's.

When the night grows dark, his mother climbs to the roof and sits next to her son.

She holds him in her arms and says, "Your father will be home soon, my dear. I promise."

And she is right.

Her husband, his father, does arrive soon. Only when he arrives, he is no longer alive.

Instead, when he returns to the planet he was born and raised on, the planet he met his wife and had kids of his own on, he arrives in a casket.

His wife and kids are at the space station when his body arrives. Once they have gathered the body, the family goes straight from the space station to the ceremony where his life is celebrated and his death mourned.

When they return home, his son makes a promise to his mother between tears.

"I will never become a Planet Explorer," he says.

But he is his father's son.

So he will break that promise, just like his father broke the promise he once made to his mother after the passing of his father, the promise that he would never become a Planet Explorer—like his father before him and his father before him and his father before him and his father before…

It was a cycle they were destined to repeat.

The Longhorns were born to explore the Universe, no matter the dangers those explorations may entail. They were born to explore the cosmos.

They were born to walk among the evilness of the Universe in search of the good that is out there.

For there is plenty of good out there.

Just waiting to be discovered.

AMBER'S

SON

THERE WERE STILL THREE MINUTES left before class was scheduled to end, but the kids were not interested in spending those final minutes learning about mathematics or science or history or English. So it did not matter how loudly their teachers yelled out—

"I did not tell you to pack up!"

Or: "The next three minutes are still mine!"

Or: "Don't forget to write down tonight's homework!"

Or: "Stay in your seats! Stay in your seats!"

—the kids continued to pack their bags and crowd in front of the door, eager for the lunch bell to dismiss them.

When the bell sounded, every door on campus flung open as a mass of children stampeded toward the cafeteria. They were serving chicken nuggets, and they all knew that the lunch ladies gave extra servings to the first five in line each day.

And that extra serving was never more valuable than on the day they served chicken nuggets.

In the front of the pack was a boy of 12 years old. His backpack, which was nearly the size of him, flapped in the wind. He was a head shorter than most, with much shorter strides than those around him.

But his legs were quick.

As he grabbed his tray and placed it down in front of the lunch ladies, securing his victory, he was huffing and puffing and smiling and looking back at his friends behind him with a pride so immense that it would last the rest of lunch. Not only did he get a larger serving than the rest, but he was also able to secure for his friends the nearest table to the counter, in case of a rare occurrence of second servings.

When the rest of his friends made it to the table, he told them all the story of how he cut the corner sharper than Tiffany's Daughter and how he saw Jasmine's Son trip over his shoelaces and how he was neck-and-neck with Octavia's Daughter for the victory and how the lunch ladies celebrated his win and how the chicken nuggets tasted extra tasty because they were so much fresher than theirs, and so on.

As they ate, his friends took turns making excuses for why they hadn't been able to beat him on that particular day.

Like: "Barbara's Daughter kept smiling at me in class so I was too distracted to pack up before the bell rang."

And: "I don't like chicken nuggets that much, so I didn't even try to win."

And: "I would have won if Debbie's Son hadn't kept pulling on my backpack to slow me down."

But no matter what their excuse was, they all said to him in the end:

"I could still beat you in a race."

So he accepted the challenge and the ultimate race was set to take place on the playground after they were done eating.

But when they went out to the playground to race, he never reached the starting line. Instead, he became distracted by a pair of boys in camouflage suits standing in front of a table covered in plastic bottles, cheap pens, brochures, stickers, and miniature flags as they yelled out at the passing students:

"Do you love your country?"

And: "Are you brave enough to serve your nation?"

And: "If so, the United States Army is the organization for you!"

He loved his country. And he had always been the bravest kid in the seventh grade. So, while the rest of his friends prepared to race, he approached the boys in camouflage suits instead.

"Hello," he said. "My mother's name is Amber. I love my country. And I'm also the bravest kid in the seventh grade. Always have been!"

He shook hands with both boys.

"My mother's name is Doris," said one.

"My mother's name is Angelica," said the other.

The sons of Doris and Angelica spent the rest of the lunch break telling the son of Amber about the time they fought in a war. They told him about how they got to fly in a plane overseas and how they got to ride in a tank and shoot guns and smoke cigarettes and drink whiskey and tell stories around the campfire and write letters home and how their commander taught them how to shave and…

"I want to go to war," said Amber's Son.

"Well," said one of the boys, "you can!"

He grabbed a piece of paper from the table and handed it to Amber's Son.

The paper had just three sentences on it. Those sentences went like this:

I hereby acknowledge that my life may be lost in war. I acknowledge that if my life is to be lost in war, it will have been lost for the greatest of causes. And, finally, I acknowledge that from this day forward, my government's enemy is eternally my enemy.

Beneath those sentences were three lines. The first line had already been signed by the Commander-in-Chief. The following lines still needed signatures.

The first signature was to come from Amber's Son. The second was to come from Amber herself.

"Here," said the other boy, grabbing a cheaply made plastic bottle with the American flag already peeling, "take this, too!"

* * *

When Amber's Son returned home, leaking bottle in hand, he was quick to put the permission slip in front of his mom.

"Mommy, Mommy," he said. "I met these soldiers at school today and they told me all about the war they were in and how they stayed in tents with all their friends and shot guns and smoked cigarettes and drank whiskey and talked to girls from the towns they visited and how they killed enemy soldiers and told stories around a campfire at night and shaved their mustaches. Can I go to war, Mommy? Please? Can I join the US Army? Please, Mommy, please! I want to help my country! I want to save America! I want to be a Patriot, Mommy! Please, oh please! I want to show the boys how brave I can be!"

Amber looked at her son and knew she hadn't a choice in her response. The answer had already been determined on her behalf. She could only go along with it now. After all, how could a mother say no to such a thing? How could a mother deny her son the right to be a Patriot? How could she not sign the paper already signed by the president of the United States? How could she not send her son to war when so many mothers had already sent theirs?

What other choice did she have?

So she picked up the pen and signed her name between the signatures of her son and the president of the United States.

Six days later, Amber's Son was in the middle of a desert in a country he could not locate on a map. Nor could he pronounce the name of the country, the people, or the language those people spoke. He hadn't a clue what the war was about or how it started. All he knew was that he was there, in that desert, to protect his countrymen back home.

Though what he was protecting them from he did not know.

His fellow soldiers varied in age. The youngest in his unit was an eight-year-old girl whose mother's name was Maya. The oldest, his commander, was seventeen.

The commander's mother's name was Heather.

"Load your guns," said Heather's Son to the other boys and girls before they departed camp for their mission through the desert.

"Keep your eyes up at all times," he said. "The enemy wants nothing more than to kill you. Don't ever forget that! The only way you can survive is to kill them first."

These were the words that echoed through the mind of Amber's Son as he crawled through the sand, slithered up and down the dunes, and followed his leader into battle.

Just last week, he had been nervously awaiting the response to the question he had asked Joyce's Daughter:

"Will you go to the seventh-grade dance with me?"

Her answer:

"Yes."

But the nerves he had felt that day, as he stood in front of Joyce's Daughter, were nothing in comparison to the nerves he felt now, as he breathed in particles of dust and swallowed the coughs he feared would give him and his fellow soldiers away.

While he crawled through the sand of this faraway land, Joyce's Daughter sat in math class, looking at the empty seat to her left, the seat that had just last week belonged to Amber's Son, the boy who was supposed to take her to the seventh-grade dance in two weeks but was now fighting in a war a million-billion miles away.

"Wait for me," Amber's Son asked of Joyce's Daughter the day before he left.

"How long will you be gone?" she asked him.

"I don't know."

"Will you be back in time for the dance?"

"I think so. How long could a war last, anyway?"

So Joyce's Daughter promised she would wait.

She promised she would say 'No' to any other boy who asked her to the dance.

She would wait for her soldier to return home from war.

She would wait...

But six days had come and gone since that conversation occurred, and she was growing more and more impatient.

After all, six days is quite a long time for a twelve-year-old kid.

Just last week, they were passing notes. Just last week, they were practicing formulas. Just last week…

But what did math matter, thought Amber's Son, if he did not have a country to practice that math in?

He needed to save his country before he could worry about the quadratic formula or the area of a circle. It was because of kids mothered by Amber, Doris, Angelica, Maya, and Heather that kids mothered by Joyce were able to learn silly mathematical formulas from the comfort of their classroom, in the comfort of their free nation.

It was that comfort Amber's Son and his fellow soldiers hoped to preserve as they crawled through the desert of that faraway land.

It was roughly four in the morning when Amber's Son was finally able to stand. They had reached the camp of the enemy and were ready to attack. They loaded their guns and reviewed once more the plan sent to them from Washington, DC—the city from which grown men and women ordered children to fight battles on their behalf in a land a million-billion miles away.

Amber's Son was assigned to the east perimeter, along with the sons and daughters of Marlaine, Freida, Savannah, Tori, Alice, Nichole, Margaret, and several others.

They stood in a straight line, looking in at a village still asleep. There were no wrinkles on any of their faces caused yet by the distresses of life. Their uniforms were all loose on their twig-like bodies. Their shoes were all a size or two too big. Their guns were nearly the height of them. And the weight of those guns caused them all to lean back just a bit to keep from falling forward.

They were just kids.

Young and innocent.

They still craved juices from boxes and milk from plastic bags. Chocolate cake for breakfast was not yet an unhealthy life decision. They still cried easily—not only from pain but also from embarrassment and anger and frustration and disappointment. They had not yet outgrown the tantrums thrown when things did not quite go according to the plans they had crafted in their minds.

They were just kids when their captain, Heather's Son, yelled, "Attack!"

They were just kids when they invaded a village filled with other kids just like them—only the uniforms they wore had different flags stitched onto their shoulders, making them their government's enemy and, therefore, eternally their enemy.

Amber's Son entered the town from the east perimeter, his gun locked and loaded, aimed forward. His head swiveled right and left as he searched for soldiers of the enemy army. The first boy he saw was even younger than he was, just nine years old. His face was panicked.

He missed his Mommy more in that moment than he ever had before.

Both of them did.

Amber's Son aimed his gun at the boy and pulled the trigger. The nine-year-old boy dropped to the ground, and Amber's Son went on looking for more soldiers to kill.

He found many.

Seven more, to be exact.

But when he came across a ninth soldier, he was not as lucky as he had been with the eight kids before. This boy, aged fourteen, was quicker to aim his gun.

And he was quicker to pull his trigger.

And this time, it was Amber's Son's turn to fall.

And this time, it was Amber's turn to mourn.

And this time…

* * *

On the same day that the body of Amber's Son was buried, the sons of Doris and Angelica were back at the school Amber's Son had attended not so long ago.

And as his old classmates ran to the playground, full of chicken nuggets, the former soldiers yelled out to them:

"Do you love your country?"

And: "Are you brave enough to serve your nation?"

And: "If so, the United States Army is the organization for you!"

A MILLION TIMES

OVER AGAIN

I HAVE ALWAYS BEEN CURIOUS about where I came from. Not in the sense of how I came to be born, but rather what circumstances came to be that made it possible for me to be born in the first place. Where did humanity come from? The animals in the forest and the fish in the sea? How did the Earth come to be formed? Who shaped our solar system? The Milky Way Galaxy? The Universe?

How did all of this—you and me, the sun and the trees— come to be?

Those are the questions that have always haunted me.

My mother says I have always been this way—curious. She says my head has always been on a swivel, looking around, searching.

I don't know what made me such a curious child. It isn't as if anybody in my family was especially curious.

My mother spent her days working at the grocery store down the street and her nights watching reality TV. My father was an insurance salesman who only sought new information when it involved his yearly search for new jobs, which never once resulted in any sort of action.

Nor were any of my siblings ever seemingly curious. None of them ever sat and pondered like I did. Or, at least, never to the depths to which my mind always seemed to be traveling.

The only things they seemed to ponder about were what their next meal was going to be, or when their next play date was, or whose house they were going to sleep over at next, or how they were going to flip their bat when they hit that inevitable home run in their next Little League game.

But not me.

While they formed friendships, I sat alone in my room. I didn't play with figurines. I didn't play make-believe. I didn't play dress-up. I didn't watch TV.

I just sat in my room, alone, with my chin in my hand—thinking.

Every time I met somebody new, I greeted them like this:

"Hi, my name is Hannah. Where do you think we came from?"

And every time, it seemed, I received an entirely new answer, a story I had never before heard.

One of my schoolmates said they came from their house via their mother's SUV. My mother said we came from God. My father said that when a daddy loves a mommy a stork delivers a baby to their front door. My sister said I came from an adoption agency upstate. My science teacher in the tenth grade said all human beings came from monkeys. The DNA test I took on my eighteenth birthday said I came from a mixture of European countries—Switzerland, Ireland, Finland, Poland, and a few others I cannot now remember. My old neighbor Steve, whom my mother told me to stay far away from and whom I nevertheless talked to on a nearly weekly basis, said we were part of an alien race, that our distant ancestors were outcasts abandoned on what was at the time a desolate planet because the planet we once lived upon had become so dangerously overpopulated that some of us had to go, our ancestors included.

The point is:

I have met many people who have given me many answers to the question—*Where do you think we came from?*

But of all the stories I have been told, of which there are thousands, none have appealed to me quite like the story my Nana told me when I was a child.

And while I have been lucky enough to savor this story as my own for all these years, it is time I share it with the world.

I think Nana would have liked that.

I was eight years old when Nana told me the story for the first time. My siblings and I had been dropped off at her house for our weekly visit while my parents tried to save their marriage with the help of a counselor.

"What a waste of fucking money, Hannah," my father told me years later, after their inevitable divorce and his second marriage. "That therapist was not interested in saving our marriage. He just wanted to keep us in a perpetual state of—"

But that's a story for another day.

On this particular afternoon, I walked up to Nana as she sat in her rocking chair, knitting a sweater, and asked, "Nana, where do you think we came from?"

I had asked her this question many times before. Usually, she brushed me away with a silly response.

But not this time.

Not that day.

"Sit," she said to me as she continued to knit.

And so I took a seat in the rocking chair next to hers.

"Hannah, dear. Why do you want so badly to know where you are from?"

"Not just me, Nana," I said. "But all of us. I want to know how we got here. I want to know where we came from. I want to know *why* we are here. I want to—What is my purpose, Nana?"

Nana stopped knitting for a moment.

She didn't look at me, though.

Instead, she stared down at the sweater. Or at her lap. Or at the ground beneath her feet.

What was going on inside of her mind, I do not know.

She remained still for several moments while I sat there with my hands crossed in my lap.

Waiting and watching.

Finally, Nana returned to her knitting.

And, without looking up, she began to answer my question.

"In the beginning," she said, "there was nothing—no trees, no wind, no rivers; no life, no cities, no societies; no suns, no moons, no galaxies; no grandkids, no mommies, no nanas; and no Universe for such things to exist within. There was just nothingness stretching toward infinity. But from that nothingness came everything that has ever existed and everything that will ever exist and everything that currently exists and everything that will never exist again. And it all started with a—"

Nana paused just long enough for me to lean forward. And then, as I moved closer still, she yelled:

"BANG!"

I jumped in my seat and giggled and waited for her to go on.

"But everything did not come immediately. Or not entirely, at least. You see, everything in existence can be attributed to that bang, as everything in this Universe, when traced back to the beginning, originates there, in that bang, flowing eternally from it, rippling evermore toward the infinity that is the Universe it helped to form. But the bang alone was not all that was needed for us to come into existence. We needed everything that came next."

I was already hanging on her every word.

"What came next, Nana?" I asked.

She paused a moment, in both her knitting and her speaking. And then, again without looking up, she continued with both.

"The creation of Souls," she said.

According to Nana, Souls came into existence just moments after the bang, when the Universe was still dark and empty and had hardly expanded more than a few inches toward the infinities around it.

She described them, Souls, as translucent beings. She declared them entirely invisible to the human eye and any technology we could ever create. She said if a Soul was standing directly in front of me, I would have no idea it was there.

I asked if there were any Souls in the room with us then, in the room we sat in as she knitted and told me her story.

"All of your questions, my dear, will be answered in the end."

And with that, she continued her story.

These Souls, though there were billions, did not have individual names. Nor did they have any differentiating factors from a physical standpoint. Instead, they were identified purely from the tonality of their essence, which individual Souls could recognize upon sight, even at incredible distances. They spoke to one another not through auditory words but through a mixture of telepathy and a thing Nana described as 'energy-reading.' They shared a connection with every other Soul in the Universe, allowing them to speak to one another despite being separated by billions of galaxies and trillions of lightyears—not through words but through a collective memory bank that gave them all access to the memories of every Soul in existence. It was as if they were all part of the same tree, each Soul serving as an individual root. They were not limited to the three simple dimensions that we human beings see in the world around us —instead, Souls saw the Universe in thousands of dimensions.

"But like Souls," said Nana, "these dimensions, though they surround us in our every moment, are unseeable with our human eyes."

In the end, the information about Souls that Nana found most important, and I found most difficult to believe with my eight-year-old mind, was this:

"Souls are uncorrupted by death. They are immortal beings. They cannot die. No matter what."

"That's impossible," I said.

"That doesn't make any sense," I said.

"That is not life as I know it to be."

Nana laughed as she continued to knit the sweater in her lap and said, "Hannah, truths don't always make sense. Reality isn't always what we wish it to be. Hypotheses are often formed only to be disproven. A fool looks at the world with preconceived expectations, never capable of understanding that anything is possible, and nothing can ever truly be understood. They believe they already know all that is possible. But we," Nana said, gesturing at herself and at me, "we are not fools in this family. Are we, my dear?"

I shook my head.

"No, Nana," I said. "We are not fools."

"That's right," said Nana. "We are not fools. And nothing is impossible."

With that, Nana continued knitting.

And telling her story.

Every Soul that has ever existed came into being at precisely the same moment.

And in the moment that followed their creation, a ceremony took place during which every freshly created Soul maneuvered their way through the still dark and otherwise empty Universe in search of their perfect mate, to whom they eternally sealed themselves. How they connected to their mate was unique to each pairing of Souls. No two connections were alike, and no one Soul could have possibly attached itself to any Soul other than the Soul the Universe had created to be their eternal mate.

"If they even so much as attempted a mating with the incorrect Soul," Nana said, as she began working on the left sleeve of the sweater, "or with an incorrect method of attachment, the entirety of the recently created Universe would have crumbled before them, returning everything to nothingness once more—making it impossible for you or me, or anything you see around us, to have ever come into existence."

But, fortunately, no such catastrophe took place, for no such attachment was improperly attempted. Every Soul knew their mate at first glance. And they sealed themselves upon sight in a way that made them and their mate no longer two individual Souls but rather a singular Soulmate, forming a bond that was so complex that it was impossible to separate them back into individual Souls.

"They were forever mated," Nana said, "never to be individuals again."

"No matter what?" I asked Nana.

"No matter what," she said.

"For quite some time," Nana went on to say, "these Souls, together with their mates, roamed the Universe. Though there wasn't much of anything for the Souls to see. You see, Hannah, the Universe was still dark. And empty. But that all changed when our Universe, in pursuit of infinite expansion, collided with a universe that existed outside our own."

"There are more universes?" I asked.

"There are infinite universes, Hannah. And each of them is as large and unique as the Universe you and I call home."

Nana proceeded to explain how our Universe collided with another, allowing for elements to flow from one universe to the next in their temporary moment of overlapping. And though the universes quickly repaired their leaks, some things were lost forever.

And other things permanently gained.

Shaking off the disturbance of two universes colliding and momentarily merging then separating once more, the Souls internally communicated with one another. They mapped out where each pair had been sent after the collision and located a centralized meeting place.

But the Souls never did make it to this agreed-upon spot. And they never did reunite. And the Universe never did recover the balance it once had before the collision.

The entire trajectory of the Universe was forever changed.

For while many elements had leaked from our Universe into the other, a very dark, very evil element had leaked into ours. And our Universe could not rid itself of it before the hole was sealed, allowing for that element to become a permanent part of our Universe. And so, as the Souls attempted to make their way to the agreed-upon location, there was an attack—or an attempted attack—on one of the flocks. The perpetrator of this attack was a dark mass made up of this evil element. A mass—in the darkness of the Universe— that the Souls were unable to see, but whose presence they could feel. And upon feeling it, they immediately dispersed. And as they dispersed, they sent a warning to the others.

"The Universe heard this warning," said Nana, "and sprung into action."

Suns exploded into existence, along with planets, which, as more and more came to be, began to cluster around the newly-born suns, forming the first-ever solar systems. And those solar systems clustered together to form galaxies. Planets continued to form, crash, intermingle, fade away, then rise again from the ashes.

Solar systems came and went. Shards of the Universe were sent in all directions, toward all infinities. Chemicals came into existence then fluttered into extinction in a matter of seconds.

And as this chaotic explosion of Universal Substance occurred, colonies of Souls began to settle upon freshly constructed planets.

To further protect these Souls, the Universe covered each planet, occupied or not, in such gases that outside observers would see a desolate planet consumed with fires and floods, ice and volcanic ash, blizzards and tornadoes, hurricanes and quakes while, on the inside, those very same gases reflected rainbows to the Souls below, rainbows that did not require storms of any sort to show off their beauty—they simply existed, every day, vibrant all the time.

Continuously, these sorts of planets came and went all across the

Universe, creating infinite galaxies filled with infinite planets all coming and going, which only helped to perpetuate the difficulties of the dark mass filled with the evil element's pursuit of Souls.

"What did the dark mass want with the Souls, Nana?"

"It wanted to destroy them," said Nana. "It wanted to once more be alone in its existence. It wanted to ensure that you and I could never exist. It wanted our Universe to itself."

"One of the planets the Souls landed on was the planet Earth. But it did not look like the Earth you know and see today. There were no McDonalds, no Taco Bells, no Starbucks, no baseball stadiums, no movie theaters, no Nana's house, no cats, no dogs, and no sweaters to stitch."

"No McDonalds?" I said, stunned, incapable of imagining such a world.

"None," said Nana.

"Not even a Starbucks?"

"Not even one."

She then went on to describe an Earth I could hardly understand, an Earth I could hardly imagine.

I looked out the window in disbelief.

"The sky was multicolored and filled with everlasting rainbows arching in all directions. The ocean below reflected the beautiful colors from the sky above, ever-changing depending on the angle of the waves, providing always unique and stunningly beautiful views. The southern edge of the Earth's singular landmass was made of towering cliffs. There were gorgeous beaches on the northern end with sand so white it glimmered in the sunlight. The grass, where it existed, was always green, the dirt always soft, the soil always fruitful, and the fruits always in season and always plentiful."

Souls efficiently used every inch of the land provided to them to build their community. And as they built, they ensured none of their infrastructure interfered with nature's integrity. They spoke to the planet and intertwined their lives with the Earth itself. They worked together perfectly, like a well-oiled machine—though machinery was a thing that did not yet exist on the planet; nor oil; only Souls and nature and rainbows and harmony. Metropolises blossomed from the ground, reaching toward the rainbow-colored sky overhead. And every constructed item was made with the cooperation of Souls and the planet itself. Trees grew in the most wonderful of shapes, flowers sprouted across the entirety of the color spectrum, and fruits bloomed in excess, yet nothing went to waste.

It was a perfect utopia made entirely of the Earth itself, occupied only by the Souls it was created to protect.

"What did the Souls do all day?" I asked Nana.

"They spent their days sitting on their porches, eating fruits and vegetables, watching as the cities around them bloomed larger and more beautiful. Or they sat on the ledge of the nearest cliff and watched as the waves turned from blue to red to purple to yellow. Or they gathered in the nearest city, large groups of Soulmates, and shared stories."

"Tell me the stories they told each other," I said.

And so Nana did.

But those stories I will keep for myself.

One day, the rainbow-colored sky went dark over the Earth as the sun overhead was covered by what appeared to be a very large, very thick cloud. However, upon further investigation, it became clear that it wasn't a cloud at all. But rather the large, dark, evil mass that the Souls of Earth had been warned about so long ago, before the Universe exploded into what we now know it to be and the diaspora of Souls to freshly constructed planets occurred.

The dark mass had the Earth, and the Souls upon it, surrounded.

I shrunk in my seat while Nana continued to knit the sweater.

"There was panic," said Nana, "among the Souls and the planet and the Universe. The Earth suddenly began to reshape itself. Holes appeared all over the planet, forming caves leading to underground tunnels. The singular landmass split into multiple pieces. Those pieces went flying in all directions. Some collided with others, forming volcanoes that immediately erupted. Soon, the Earth looked like every other planet in the Universe did from the outside looking in—a place of chaos, panic, and fear. The planet continued to contort itself until all the Souls had been safely secured within, the Earth covering them with water and mountains and layers of soil and grass and rocks and volcanic ash…"

But the dark mass, foreign to our Universe, was undeterred in its pursuit of the Souls of Earth.

In the end, it did not matter where they hid, how deeply they were buried within the Earth, what lengths the Universe went to further cover them up, the dark mass found every Soul. And when it did, like a vacuum, it pulled the Souls into itself.

"What was inside the dark mass?" I asked Nana.

"Little creatures," said Nana. "Creatures that were the antithesis of Souls."

"What does that word mean, Nana? An-ti-ti-tis?"

"Antithesis, dear. It means they are the opposite of Souls."

"Like evil Souls?"

"The evilest."

Once every Soul had been pulled inside, a war was waged. There was a piercing scream that came from deep within the belly of the mass. Lightning bolts launched from it, striking the ground below, causing the oceans to roar, lakes to overflow, rainbows to fade. Cities crumbled, gardens withered, homes flooded, mountains toppled. The land masses that made up the planet Earth, already split into pieces, split furthermore.

Then the screaming stopped.

The storming ceased.

And for a moment there was stillness—nothing more than a dark mass floating above the surface of a now desolate and colorless planet. All signs of the utopia that once existed not so long ago had been entirely erased. All signs of such a world had been completely washed away.

The dark mass opened, releasing thousands of Souls, no longer attached to their mates, to the Earth below. And as quickly as the dark mass had come, it went away, in search of other planets housing more Souls still connected to their mates, still living upon their own utopian planets, in hopes of doing to them the same it had just done to the Souls of Earth.

With the departure of the dark mass, sunlight returned to the Earth, upon which there was now no color and no movement. For billions of years, this is how the Earth remained: motionless and desolate, with millions of Souls ripped away from their mates, lying on the surface of the now-destroyed planet, unable to move.

Yet, Souls are immortal beings. So, without their mates, they were left to live an eternal life of immobility and loneliness on a planet once filled with beauty, now severed and destroyed. They were unable even to speak to the other Souls on the planet with them. Even if they lay beside each other, it was as if they were universes apart.

Nor were they able to converse with their fellow Souls across the Universe, to warn them or otherwise—for, apart from their mates, their internal wirings had been ripped to shreds and their connections destroyed.

"What happened to the Souls?" I asked.

Nana did not answer immediately.

Instead, she sat there, patiently knitting, working hard on the right sleeve of the sweater, before finally clearing her throat and saying, "While the Earth had been weakened, while it was tired and broken, like the Souls still lying upon it, the Earth was not defeated. There was still energy within it, buried deep, almost nonexistent— but it was there. And with that little bit of energy, the planet gave birth to the first form of life ever seen on Earth. It did so in the ocean which, even after billions of years, still rocked from the storm caused by the visitation of the dark mass. This life form, a single-cell organism, slowly evolved over billions of years into something Souls could use to guide them back to their mate."

Nana, once more, had me on the edge of my seat.

The creatures that spawned from this single-cell organism grew into all sorts of species of all shapes and sizes. They grew legs and arms and fins and teeth. Then, one day, growing tired of the sea, one of the life forms escaped the water and wandered onto land. And so, within the sea and upon the land, the experiments continued: new creatures, new shapes, new sizes, new diets, new societies, new habitats.

Until eventually came a species that stood upright on two legs with two arms dangling by its side.

"This creature," said Nana, "the first of its kind, came across a magical tree. And on that tree, it discovered a dangling fruit. The creature, quite hungry, grabbed the fruit from the tree and bit into it. Do you know what fruit it was, Hannah?"

I shook my head.

"It was an apple."

According to Nana, the juices from the apple flowed through the mouth of the creature and into its bloodstream. That blood flowed through the body and into the creature's brain. It was in the brain that the magic took place: for the juice from the apple quite literally reshaped the brain, creating in it a little crevice.

"This newly created crevice in the brain of this creature," said Nana, "just so happened to be the exact same size as a Soul. And a Soul just so happened to be lying by the side of this magical tree."

* * *

The Soul lying by the tree had been there for billions of years, unable to move since it had been dropped in that location by the dark mass.

But suddenly, as the creature stood over it, eating this magical apple, reshaping its brain within, the wirings of the Soul, which it once used to latch to its mate, began to tingle. And as the creature took bite after bite, the wirings lifted in the direction of the creature, until suddenly the Soul found itself standing, moving toward the creature. And with each step, the Soul grew increasingly stronger and determined in its pursuit.

The Soul, following an intuition it did not fully understand, grabbed onto the left leg of the creature and climbed—up its leg, onto its waist, its stomach, chest, neck, face, and then finally onto its nose, where the Soul then slithered inside the right nostril.

Once inside, the Soul discovered the newly created crevice inside the creature's brain, where standing erect were wires similar to its own. So the Soul, growing more curious with each passing moment, tinkered with its wires and the internal wirings of the brain it now found itself inside.

It took this wire and wrapped it around that part of the brain, it took that wire and wrapped it around this, and so on and so forth, until suddenly the Soul felt a new strength, a new power, a new connection—not quite as strong as the connection it once had billions of years before, when it was attached to its mate, but a connection that was still incredibly strong.

It was a bond that was inseparable, unbreakable, except for the occurrence of one thing: the death of the creature whose brain it was now connected.

Furthermore, the connection was not strong enough for the Soul to force the creature to move this way or the other. It could not use this connection to change the way the creature inherently thought. It could not do anything other than whisper ideas to the creature's subconscious, wait as those thoughts festered over a duration of time, and slowly inspire the creature to act in a way it did not always understand, following an inkling in its mind whose source could not be found.

"And, just like that," said Nana, "the first human being on Earth had found its Soul."

"That creature," I said. "It was a human?"

"It was."

"Like you and me?"

"That's right, Hannah. A human being like you and me."

I began to ponder. I wondered about this, and I wondered about that. And then, finally, I asked, "Is there a Soul inside of me, Nana? Is there a Soul inside of you?"

Nana laughed.

"Patience, my dear," she said. "As I have stated before, all of your questions will be answered in the end."

And with that, Nana continued her story.

For years, that first human being, following the guidance of an influence it did not understand, provided by a Soul within that it did not know existed, wandered the Earth in search of a thing it could not see, with no awareness of what it was looking for. It wandered valleys, mountains, riverbanks, and coastlines, chasing a thing it did not know it chased; feeling an emptiness, a longing it could never satisfy despite how hard it tried to do so. And when this human being was, in the end, incapable of finding what the Soul within so desperately desired, it collapsed.

And the human being died.

With this death, the connection that kept the Soul in place—in the crevice of this human's brain—was broken, as the wirings of the human being were no longer strong enough to contain the Soul. And so the Soul was expelled from the body, dropped back to the dust it had spent so much of its existence in, where it remained next to the body, which slowly rotted and faded into oblivion until it was nothing more than bones and fragments of food for the larva of Earth to slowly consume.

Until, once more, with the larva now gone, the Soul was alone.

That Soul remained there in the dirt for centuries, until finally another human—which too had evolved to the state of having the same crevice in its brain—came near enough to give that Soul the strength to stand and latch itself within.

Once inside the brain, the Soul slowly and painstakingly and exhaustively influenced that human body to further roam the Earth —taking it into deeper valleys, up higher mountains, across wider riverbanks, along longer coastlines.

This continued, the influencing of this second human body in search of its mate, until that human body also grew tired, sick, weak, and eventually fell to its death, expelling the Soul once more to the dust, causing the cycle to begin anew.

Again, and again, and again.

But as the Soul cycled through dozens and then hundreds and then thousands of human bodies, it did not grow weary, it did not grow dejected, and it did not grow hopeless. It remained through it all optimistic that it would one day be reunited with its mate.

Even if it took millions of years—billions! trillions!

The Soul had time.

It had infinite time.

"Then one day," said Nana, "the Soul located its mate bodiless in a lake, submerged beneath several feet of water. The human that housed the Soul within saw nothing with its human eyes, but the Soul could see its mate, even beneath all that water. To the Soul, its mate glowed. The light of its presence radiated from hundreds of yards away. The Soul influenced the body to go towards the lake.

And with each step the body took toward the Soul's long-lost mate, the stronger grew the Soul's influencing powers over the body. And so, even while the body, which was terribly afraid of drowning, did not want to get any deeper into the lake than it already was, a voice within, now screaming, convinced it otherwise—until the body was nearly neck deep in the water."

Nana was no longer knitting.

Instead, she was standing. She was speaking triumphantly. She gestured the steps the Soul forced the human body to take with great exaggeration—her knees nearly hitting her chest, her arms swinging high and wide, her chest sticking out as far as it would go.

"The Soul within demanded that the body stop directly in front of its mate." Nana gestured a dramatic stop. "The Soul attempted desperately to unlatch itself and undo the wires that connected it to the brain. But the Soul quickly remembered what it had learned long ago: that it was impossible to unlatch from a human body that was still alive—for in the process of sealing itself to the brain of the human being it had formed a connection that could not be voluntarily terminated. So the Soul within, just inches away from its long-lost mate, could do nothing but influence the human to reach, confusedly, toward the mate in hopes of grabbing it, picking it up, and placing it next to the Soul that already occupied its mind. However, the hand simply went into its mate and through it."

This, too, Nana mimed. She knelt down in the middle of the living room and reached out her hand. She swept the top of the carpet and came up empty-handed. She did this a few more times, growing more and more despondent with each attempt.

Then:

"The Soul had a sudden idea," said Nana. "It influenced the body to stand and begin to dance."

Nana too began to dance in the funkiest way imaginable. She kicked her feet in the air and flapped her arms. Then she bounced on one foot, spun in circles, rapidly touched her fingertips to her nose, ear, chest, eye, knee, then back to her nose. She clapped her hands, banged her chest, made wild noises with her tongue and lips. She breathed rapidly and whistled and screamed and whispered gibberish. She wiggled her toes and fingers. She kicked forward and backward, touched her heels, kissed her elbows.

I laughed so hard in my seat that I nearly peed myself.

"Stop it, Nana," I said. "Stop it, stop it! I'm going to pee, I'm going to pee!"

But she did not stop until I rolled off my seat and raced to the bathroom.

Once I returned, I asked her, "What did that silly dance mean, Nana?"

"To the body that performed the dance," Nana said, "it meant nothing. But to the Soul within, and to the Soul beneath the water, it meant, 'It's me, your mate.' It meant, 'I found you.' It meant, 'I am inside this human body.' It meant, 'I am going to find you your own human body.' It meant, 'When I find you that body, I need you to latch yourself to its brain, located here, through this nostril.' It meant, 'I am going to leave you now, but I promise I am going to return.' It meant, 'I found you. I finally found you.'"

Finished with its dance, the Soul influenced the body to turn and run out of and away from the lake, which wasn't so hard to do considering the body had been aching to leave ever since its strange arrival. The body and the Soul within ran toward some smoke in the distance, smoke that could indicate only one thing—the presence of human beings.

When the body returned to the lake, it was no longer alone. It guided its new partner by the shoulders, moving it as needed to the left and right, forward and backward.

"Right there," it said.

The Soul within the lake, with wires now fully erect, began to climb up the body and toward the face. It slithered its way into the right nostril as instructed and into the little crevice inside of its brain. Then, after a moment's silence, the two bodies embraced.

And the mating of these two Souls—thanks to these two human bodies—though not nearly as strong as it once was before, had been reignited.

"For years," said Nana, "these two human bodies were inseparable. Where one went, the other followed."

This continued until one of the bodies got sick. Knowing this was a sign that death was near, the healthy human whispered to the Soul of the other, "I will find you another human body. And I will continue to find you bodies a million times over again. I will find humans without a Soul and bring them to you so that we can be together again. I promise, my love. I promise. A million times over again…a million times over again."

With this promise understood, the body died.

And the Soul within was expelled.

At this point in the telling of her story, Nana had finished stitching the sweater.

She lifted it up and examined it closely, inch by inch.

"Here," she said to me, "try this on."

So I did.

And as I did, Nana said:

"That, Hannah, is where we came from. We are the gift provided by Earth for the Souls it was built to protect. That is why we seek, with such fervor, love in all that we do: for we are, in actuality, influenced by an inner Soul in its everlasting pursuit of its eternal mate."

The sweater fit perfectly, though it was incredibly itchy. I fought the desire to scratch, then lost.

And as I scratched all over, I asked, "Where do you think my Soulmate is, Nana?"

Nana smiled, "Isn't it clear, my dear?"
I shook my head.
"It's right here," said Nana, pointing at herself.
"You?"
"Me."

I didn't believe her at first.

I thought she was just being silly.

Telling jokes.

Making funnies.

But I no longer think that.

Now, I know she was telling the truth.

You see, two years ago, Nana passed away from cancer. I knew of her passing before the call came. At the very moment she died, I felt a sudden weakness come over my body. A weakness that forced me to immediately sit down.

Instantly, I had a headache.

And a thought.

"Nana," I said to myself.

I thought back to the last time I had seen her, which was just a few days prior to her passing. She was lying in bed, bald and weak. There was a tube flowing oxygen through her nostrils. She had a pulse oximeter on her finger. There was a needle in her arm slowly feeding her chemicals.

For the three days I was there, she did not say a word. She did not as much as open her eyes.

She was, so it seemed, in a vegetative state.

"Any day now," the doctor kept saying to me.

"Say your goodbyes," she said.

"While she can still hear you."

And so I did.

I sat at her bedside and held her hand, which was incredibly cold. I told her that I loved her. I thanked her for everything she had done for me as a child and young adult. I told her I would cherish her stories forever.

And I told her I would find her again.

"A million times over again," I said.

Those were the last words I ever said to her.

At least, those were the last words I said to her while she was still inside the human body that represented my Nana.

But I know I will see her again.

A million times over again.

It Was Just Another Day in America

IT WAS JUST ANOTHER DAY in America when Jasper's mother woke him up for school. He got out of bed. He showered. He dressed in the clothes laid out for him. Then he went downstairs and ate a bowl of cereal.

On the counter, waiting for him before he walked out to the bus, was a blue and yellow lunch pail filled with a peanut butter and jelly sandwich with the crust cut off, a sliced-up apple, a small bottle of water, and a bag of baby carrots.

His mother walked him to the door. She held in her hand a thick leaden vest.

As she knelt before him, she asked, "Do you remember the combination to your bunker?"

He held his arms up as his mother slid the vest over his head and nodded.

"What is it?" she asked, buckling the vest across his chest as she did.

"17-24-8-19-22."

"And what do you do when you get inside?"

"I don't say a word."

"That's right. You don't say a word."

The bus pulled up outside.

"Be safe, okay?"

"I know, mom. I know."

She kissed him on the cheek and told him she loved him.

"Say it back," she said as she tickled him all over. "Say it back, say it back, say it back."

And so he did—though he did it quietly and without eye contact.

"I love you, too."

His mother kissed him again on the cheek and pushed him out the door, toward the bus.

She watched him as he went.

Praying she would get to see him again.

On the bus, every kid wore a vest similar to his. As did the bus driver. On the dashboard, hidden behind a thin layer of glass, was an emergency gun.

That gun was loaded at all times.

Jasper walked silently to the back of the bus, where he sat alone. It wasn't until the seventh stop that a friend finally arrived. Jasper sat up excitedly at the sight of him and waved his hand and patted the seat next to him.

"Hi, Bryan," said Jasper, though thanks to his speech impediment, his Rs sounded more like Ws.

"Hi, Jasper," said Bryan.

Bryan and Jasper had been friends for as long as they could remember. Sometimes they called each other cousins. Other times, they called each other brothers.

During the ride to school, they talked about all their favorite things: Star Wars and basketball and trading cards and video games. They told each other jokes they had come up with the night before and stories they had shared every day but never grew tired of and traded opinions on last night's episode of their favorite show and...

It was just another day in America.

When they arrived at school, they joined the back of the line for security. When they reached the front, they removed their backpacks and slid them, along with their lunch pails, through the X-ray scanner. They lifted their arms and split their legs as a police officer scanned them from head to toe.

On hearing the word 'Clear', they moved forward and grabbed their backpacks and lunch pails. There was still time before school was set to begin, so Jasper and Bryan ran to their classroom to put their belongings in their cubbies. Other students were standing by the cubbies when they arrived but these students did not say hello to Bryan or Jasper. Nor did Bryan or Jasper say hello to them. Jasper was glad about this. For when the others did talk to him, they often called him names like 'Four-Eyes' or 'Soulless Ginger' or 'Chubby Fingers' or 'Curly Whirly' or 'St-st-st-stuttering Ja-ja-ja-jasper'…

After setting their belongings in their cubbies, they ran to the playground and joined the back of the line for four-square and waited their turn. But their turn never came. Instead, the bell rang and the kids were forced to stop the game and make their way to class.

Mrs. Smith stood at the door and welcomed each student as they entered.

"Good morning," she said.

"Great to see you again," she said.

"Welcome back," she said.

The desks were organized in groups of five, except for one group, which was made up of only two desks.

Those were Jasper's and Bryan's desks.

Mrs. Smith had tried many other arrangements before this but had found this was the only way to limit the bullying.

The school day began, as it always did, with students being ordered to stand by an omnipresent voice over the loudspeaker.

"Everybody stand," demanded that voice.

"Place your hand over your heart," the voice said next.

"Ready? And begin."

Together, in one voice, the entirety of the school—students and teachers and faculty members—pledged their eternal allegiance to the United States of America.

The country of the free and the brave.

The country that God watched over endlessly.

Only after they had all finished their pledge were their school lessons allowed to begin.

Mrs. Smith started the class by reviewing their vocabulary for the week. Next, they practiced writing in cursive. They were then grouped by reading levels and assigned stories to read.

As always, Bryan and Jasper were placed together as the highest-reading duo in the class. They read a book about a tortoise who learned that speed was not as important as having the endurance to finish the race.

"I bet I could beat you in a race," said Jasper once they had finished their reading.

"Nuh-uh," Bryan argued. "I am faster than a cheetah."

"Oh, yeah?" said Jasper. "Well, I am faster than light."

"That's impossible!"

"No, it's not!"

"Uh-huh!"

"Nuh-uh!"

During recess, the playground was surrounded by police officers and soldiers. They kept their backs to the children and their eyes straight ahead. They held their guns at the ready, knowing there would be no time to waste should an intruder enter school grounds.

The nation had lost too many children already.

But Jasper and Bryan hardly noticed the officers, the soldiers, the guns, the helicopters overhead, the towers, or anything else intended to keep them safe.

They cared only about the four-square court they sprinted to, determined that this time they would get their chance to play.

First, it was Jasper. He stepped into the fourth square, bent his knees, and readied for the serve. The girl in square-one hit it to square-three, who hit it to square-two, who hit it back to square-one, who hit it back to square-three, who hit it into the corner of square-four. Jasper reached out with his left hand. He saw the angles perfectly in his mind. He knew exactly how hard he needed to hit the ball and where he needed to hit it and how he needed to angle his wrist to perfectly place the ball in the corner of the first square and knock her out of the game.

But that was the easy part: the math. The hard part was getting his body to do what it needed to do. And so, instead of perfectly hitting the ball on the left side of his left palm, he missed the ball entirely. He went tumbling down to the asphalt. The ball went past him. He scraped his knee. He rolled over, getting dirt all over his back. Rocks stuck to his vest and when he stood, he had to slap them away.

"B-b-b-b-back of the line," said the girl in the first square.

"Yeah," said the boy in second, "b-b-back of the line, Jasper the Nerdy Ghost."

He went to the back of the line as those around him laughed at his expense. Taking his place in the fourth square was Bryan, who hoped to have more success than his friend.

He bent his knees, squinted his eyes, and prepared the math in his head.

After recess, as she did every day, Mrs. Smith taught the kids about a special time in history. This was always Jasper's favorite part of the day. He was fascinated with the ancient world, old societies, and forgotten cultures. He loved to learn about the ways human beings once lived.

On this particular day, they learned about nomads.

"I want to be a nomad," Bryan whispered to Jasper as Mrs. Smith taught. He talked about how he wanted to roam the world, see different sites, meet other people. He wanted to chase animals. He wanted to build temporary settlements only to tear them down days later and begin anew.

As part of an activity following the lesson on nomads, Mrs. Smith ordered the students to move their desks from the center of the room to the perimeters to free up space. Next, they were given sticks, ropes, cardboard boxes, blankets, and pillows. With this material, along with the desks and chairs and textbooks and any other classroom item they could find, the students were put into pairs and instructed to build temporary homes.

While the rest of the kids ran around the room, grabbing whatever they could get their hands on and frantically beginning to build, Jasper and Bryan sat back. They formulated a plan. They took paper and pen and drew out their ideas. They talked about mathematics and physics. They considered usability along with aesthetics. They watched the forts crumbling around them and laughed. Then, with a clear plan in mind, they began to build. They took a couple of desks and put them in position. They took some sticks and placed them where they needed to be. Then they went to grab—

DIIIIIIIIIIIIIIIIIIIIIIIIIIIIIIIING! DIIIIIIIIIIIIIIIIIIIIIIIIIIIIIING! DIIIIIIIIIIIIIIIIIIIIIIIIIIIIIIIIIIING!

Students knew immediately what to do at the sound of those three long dings. They had heard them many times throughout the school year. They dropped their blankets, their pillows, their chairs, their cardboard boxes. They pushed over their freshly constructed forts and sprinted to the back of the class, to their assigned bunkers. These bunkers looked like lockers, only large enough for a tiny child to squeeze inside. Each student entered the combination assigned to them at the beginning of the school year.

After locking the door, Mrs. Smith broke the glass behind her desk and grabbed the emergency gun. She watched as the kids continued to enter their combinations, for she was not allowed to enter her bunker until every student had entered theirs.

Bunker doors opened and kids climbed inside. But not every student remembered their combination. Some were left standing there, staring at the flashing red lights indicating a wrong password had been entered. Their eyes filled with panic.

"Mrs. Smith!" they yelled.

"I don't remember my password!" they cried.

"Help me! Help me! Help me!"

But teachers were no longer given access to the combinations of their students' bunkers ever since one teacher in Arkansas had used them to slaughter her entire class.

All Mrs. Smith could do now was order them to call their mothers or fathers and keep trying to remember.

Jasper entered his combination—17-24-8-19-22—and turned to watch the frantic class: kids crying as they called their parents, Mrs. Smith standing in front of the class with her loaded gun, students climbing into bunkers. He could hear gunshots getting closer, screams, cries, threats, and promises. He heard bodies falling to the floor outside. He heard demands being yelled by police officers and infiltrators.

He wanted to help. He wanted to help everybody, but there was nothing he could do.

And so, with guilt in his heart, he climbed inside his bunker and closed the door behind him.

The world went silent within.

He grabbed one of the coloring books he had stored inside to keep himself occupied, along with a box of markers. He opened the book and flipped through the pages.

Nearly all of the animals inside had already been colored in—at first haphazardly, and then again with detail.

He found a lion near the back which had only been colored over once, and got to work, trying hard to forget about the world outside his bunker.

* * *

Jasper was inside that bunker for nearly two hours before a police officer finally unlocked it. When he exited, there were blood stains scattered around the class, but no bodies to give any indication of who the blood had come from.

It wasn't until all of the students had been removed from their bunkers and returned to their seats that Jasper and the others learned who had been lost.

All around the class, groups of 5 had been turned into groups of 4, 3, 2, or even 1. A substitute teacher was needed to cover for the rest of the day. And the seat to Jasper's left was now empty of his best friend.

"I am sorry for the disturbance," said the omnipresent voice over the speaker once all had been settled. "But our school day is now clear to resume."

It was just another day in America.

PREPARING

TO DIE

THE SUN HAD ONLY JUST begun to peak through the windows when a little white Yorkshire Terrier jumped onto the bed and began to scratch at its owner. When the initial scratching proved ineffective, the dog added in a little whining. And when that whining was still not enough, the dog began to bark.

Yap! Yap! Yap! Yap! Yap!

Until:

"Okay! Okay! I'm up."

With this, the old man rolled over and the dog moved in toward his face, wagging her tail speedily as she licked him.

"Good morning to you too, Charlie," said the old man, laughing, moving his head to and fro in a failed attempt to avoid her tongue.

As the old man sat up, Charlie jumped off of the bed and ran to the bedroom door, which was still closed.

She turned back to the old man and wagged her tail and gave another quick bark.

Yap!

"I'm coming, Charlie. I'm coming."

The old man opened the door for Charlie and she went running into the kitchen. First, she drank some water. Then she ate a bit of food. Then she stretched a bit. Then she drank some more water. Then she ate some more food.

The old man exited the bedroom a few minutes later, dressed in an all-grey sweatsuit. As he poured himself a thermos of coffee,

Charlie ran to the front door, where her leash and harness hung, and barked some more.

Yap! Yap! Yap! Yap! Yap!

The old man let Charlie run down the three flights of stairs on her own as he waited for the elevator. When the elevator door opened on the other side, Charlie was sitting there waiting for him. Her tail wagged behind her as the elevator opened and revealed the old man. She immediately rolled onto her back and the old man bent down to rub her belly.

"Good girl. Good girl."

Once Charlie deemed herself satisfied, she jumped back on all fours and ran toward the nearest bush for some inquisitive smells.

As she sniffed, two young women walked by in bright neon sweatsuits. It was the same two women they saw every morning on their walks, but the old man could never remember their names.

"Good morning, Cody," they said to him.

"And good morning to you too, Charlie," they added as they passed.

Cody and Charlie took the same route every morning. Charlie smelled the same bushes, peed in the same spots, pooped on the same lawn, and barked at the same garden gnome she barked at every day.

When they neared the flight of stairs, Cody let Charlie go and headed towards the...

Three blurry figures stood over Cody, becoming slightly clearer each time he blinked, until they all took shape as familiar figures from around the complex, though Cody didn't know a single one of their names.

Charlie was barking at each of them, one after the other, warning them to step away but also asking them to help. Then she directed her attention to Cody, demanding he stand back up:

Yap! Yap! Yap! Yap! Yap!

"Mr. Wettenberg, sir, are you okay?" asked one of the blurry, unnamed neighbors.

Yap! Yap! Yap! Yap! Yap!

"What happened?" said Cody.

"You were standing by the elevator and then you just—"

Yap! Yap! Yap! Yap! Yap!

"Oh, Charlie, won't you shut up? I'm fine!"

Charlie immediately stopped barking, switching instead to licking Cody's face, slobbering all over him.

Cody tried to sit but immediately became dizzy and fell back down. He closed his eyes and held his head and tried to push Charlie away but eventually gave up. Charlie had always been persistent when it came to licking faces. Especially Cody's. Besides, the saliva was starting to cool him down. So he permitted it.

Then he embraced it.

"Jodi," said a man now kneeling over Cody, "call 9-1-1."

"No," said Cody. He opened his eyes and tried to sit up, mumbling something about insurance and how he couldn't...

He passed out again.

"Cancer," said the doctor. The sort of cancer that, if spotted earlier, could have been easily treated. But it wasn't caught earlier. Instead, it had been caught late. Very late. Too late. And as a result, it could no longer be treated easily.

In fact, it couldn't be treated at all.

The doctor said he had only a month to live. Maybe two, if he was lucky.

"Two months, eh?" said Cody. "How lucky am I ."

"Some aren't so lucky," said the doctor. "Some are dead before they even know they are dying."

Cody mumbled something under his breath about luck and death.

After a moment, the doctor went on:

"I would suggest you get your—uhm—your things in order...

while you still have the time…and the energy."

He fumbled through the top drawer of his desk, pulled out a business card, and slid it toward Cody. Cody picked up the card but did not say a word. He looked at the card, read the front, flipped it over, read the back, and then looked up at the doctor.

"He's really great," said the doctor. "I recommend him to all my patients who are…well…"

"Dying?"

The doctor didn't respond.

After a moment, Cody stood, pocketed the card, and left.

Cody filled Charlie's food and water before pouring himself a glass of whiskey. As he drank, he stared at the card. It was rather plain, having only a photo, a job title, and a phone number. The photo was of a young man, no older than 25. He had a mustache, horn-rimmed glasses, and slicked-back blonde hair. His job title was the Death Coordinator.

Cody grabbed his phone and dialed the number.

"Why, hi there! You have reached the Death Coordinator, where death is made just a little bit easier. How may I help you?"

The voice of the Death Coordinator was so joyful, so energetic, so innocent that Cody lost all of the words he had rehearsed in his head.

"Why, hi there. You have reached the Death Coordinator," said the same voice, though with a little less certainty, "where death is made just a little bit easier. How may I help you?"

Cody lifted the whiskey to his lips and took a sip. He watched Charlie as she ate.

Then finally he said, "My name is Cody Wettenberg. I am seventy-two years old. And I—and I just found out I have only a month to live—two months if…if I'm lucky."

"Two months, huh? Wow…Well…that is just *wonderful* news, Cody! You have called me at the perfect time. Perfect! Two months gives us plenty of time to coordinate your death. Most people don't call me until after they are dead. Or, well, they don't call me. A loved one does. And they ask me to coordinate their entire death in just a couple of days, which isn't an issue—after all, I am the best Death Coordinator in town. Ask anyone! But two months—Cody, is it?—two months will give us a lot of time to, well, to have some fun. Now, Cody, tell me, do you have a spouse?"

"I do not."

"Kids?"

"None."

"I see, I see."

Cody could hear the Death Coordinator typing on the other end of the phone.

"Now, Cody, tell me, what do you know about Death Coordinators?"

"I know that you—uhm—coordinate things," said Cody. "And I assume what you coordinate has one thing or another to do with death."

"That's funny," said the Death Coordinator. And you could tell from the tone of his voice that he truly meant it. "That's good, you know. To still have your sense of humor. Death isn't easy, but humor makes it easier—that, and Death Coordinators. That's what I always say. I say, Death isn't easy, but humor and Death Coordinators make it easier. It's true."

And it was true.

He did say it often.

"As you have said," the Death Coordinator went on, "my job is to coordinate. And what I coordinate has something to do with death. You see, most people think dying is easy. But it isn't. There is so much that needs to be done even after you are dead. For starters, what do we do with your body? Do we cremate it or bury it? Do we stuff your ashes in an urn, a wall, or pour them out in the park—and if so, which park? Should we turn those ashes into a necklace? Or how about a ring? They can really do anything these days when it comes to ashes. And if you want to be buried, then where do you want to be buried? And in what sort of casket? And your stuff— your home, your belongings, your money—what do we do with it all? And—"

"You're hired," said Cody, interrupting the Death Coordinator with his listing of things that needed to be done.

"Pardon?"

"You can coordinate my death. Just tell me where to go and I will be there."

"Oh, boy, Cody, that is just *wonderful* news. Yes, sir. I am going to—I promise! No! I guarantee!—I am going to make this death so easy for you that you'll wish you could die twice!"

"I'm sure I will," said Cody, patting Charlie on the stomach. "Listen," he added, "wherever we go, I need to take Charlie."

"I see, I see…and who exactly is Charlie?"

Cody was surprised to find that the Death Coordinator looked even younger in person. As they went through the usual pleasantries, he loosely constructed the premise of a joke in his mind based on the novel *Dorian Grey* by Oscar Wilde. Something about how the Death Coordinator was actually an extremely old man, but appeared young because he feasted on the remaining life of his customers, giving him eternal youth and his customers eternal death. But he struggled to find a smart or witty way of doing so, and before long the joke had fallen apart.

"Before we get into the fun," said the Death Coordinator, "it is important that we get some logistics out of the way. After all, as you recently have been made painfully aware, tomorrow is no longer— uhm—well—it is no longer a guarantee."

He looked up at Cody but did not get a response. He cleared his throat and continued.

"For legal purposes, it is important that we get your will out of the way. I would like to start by first considering your largest possessions—your house, your car, any collectibles or high-value items. Things of that nature."

"No need," said Cody. "I want to give everything away."

"Well, the thing is—"

"Except for one thing," Cody interjected. "Her."

Charlie looked up at him as if she knew she was being talked about. She lifted her head and dropped it right next to Cody's hand, glancing at it until it was finally lifted and rubbed against her.

After Charlie's fate had been determined and the will had been written and every signature had been acquired, the Death Coordinator placed the will in his filing cabinet.

"Now that that's out of the way," said the Death Coordinator, walking to the bookcase across the room, "it is time for the fun: planning your dream funeral."

The shelves were filled with binders. The Death Coordinator rubbed his hand against the spines, reading over the codes that Cody could not decipher, and selected three.

He set the three on the table.

"Here are three clients who had very similar preferences to the ones you have shared with me. However, they had three extremely different budgets. I prefer to show my clients what each spending tier can get them before they decide on their own budget. That seem fair to you?"

Cody nodded.

"Wonderful. So, this client here," said the Death Coordinator, placing his hand on the first binder, "spent about thirty thousand. While this client spent about six thousand. And this client spent roughly eighteen thousand."

"Jesus," said Cody, "it'd be cheaper to just stay alive."

The Death Coordinator laughed hysterically, which startled Charlie and caused her to bark loudly—

Yap! Yap! Yap! Yap! Yap!

This quickly stopped the Death Coordinator's laughter. He straightened up and adjusted his tie and cleared his throat and then spoke very seriously, taking Cody through each binder, page after page.

He provided Cody with his opinions of each page, the reviews from his customers, some much-needed facts, the price points of each particular item, and so on. He went over every necessary detail and thought deeply before he spoke. He made sure Cody understood everything he said before he turned to the next page.

With a clear budget now in mind, along with a deeper understanding of the type of funeral Cody hoped to have, the Death Coordinator took Cody and Charlie to a part of the city they had never seen before. There were warehouses in all directions, yet no clear signage to differentiate one from the other. Abandoned cars, windowless and tireless, were scattered through the streets. In the alleys, men and women rested beneath shredded tarps. There was no greenery in sight, only dirt and scraps of metal and rubber from torn-apart tires and loose piles of trash and concrete slabs partially torn from the ground.

"Here we are," said the Death Coordinator as he pulled into a small parking lot. "*Caskets, Urns, and More*, home to the largest selection of caskets this side of the Mississippi. And more!"

A young kid greeted them at the door. He wore a yellow shirt with two vertical red stripes and a name tag that said: *Hello, my name is Tony*. His pants were red, as were his shoes.

"Good afternoon," said Tony in a monotone. "Welcome to *Caskets, Urns, and More*, where the dead come to rest peacefully. How may I aid in your mourning process?"

But before Cody or the Death Coordinator could respond, Charlie took it upon herself to let this young kid know exactly how he could help.

Yap! Yap! Yap! Yap! Yap!

"Charlie," said Cody. "You stop that right now."

But Charlie did not stop. She only barked louder as she lunged forward and attempted to bite the young kid. The kid, however, did not flinch. He just stood there, staring and blinking. Almost wishing to be bit.

Anything to get a day off of work.

Or even a couple of hours.

Cody pulled Charlie away as he followed the Death Coordinator into the warehouse, past the young kid who didn't seem to care that they were walking away.

The warehouse was filled with thousands of caskets separated into dozens of categories that Cody had never before associated with caskets. Up until that point, he thought all caskets were built the same. After all, what difference did it make to a dead body what the casket was made of, how it was shaped, or what artwork was included?

And yet, there were thousands of possibilities. Tens of thousands. Each with its own subtle design.

There were caskets made of mahogany, walnut, cherry, maple, oak, or pine. Some used gold, others silver, some bronze. Some were half-couch, while others were full-couch. Then there were the various interior designs, including the pillows and blankets and choice of linen. Some had sayings stitched inside the casket for the dead to read during their eternal rest, while others had sayings etched into the exterior for the entertainment of worms.

Cody looked over each casket. He studied their designs. He felt their linen. He pressed his palms against the pillows and judged their softness.

"Get in," said the Death Coordinator.

"What?"

"Try them on for size."

So, he did. He climbed in casket after casket. He lay this way, then that. He closed his eyes and carefully listened to every inch of his body. And after thirty or forty caskets, he decided on the one.

The Death Coordinator was ecstatic about the decision. He grabbed one of the cards from the casket's pouch as Cody climbed out. The card had all the information the cashier would need to order Cody the proper casket in time for his upcoming passing.

"Now," said the Death Coordinator, handing the card to Cody, "let's go look at some flowers."

By the time they made it to the cash register, Cody had accumulated a thick stack of cards indicating his selection of wreaths, picture frames, easels, bouquets, candles, linens, pallbearer gloves, and several other things. He set them on the counter and the cashier, wearing the same uniform as the young kid up front, grabbed them and studied them one by one.

"Oh, boy," she said, "these are some truly beautiful picks."

She then looked up at Cody and said, "I am so sorry for your loss, sir."

Before Cody could respond, the Death Coordinator interrupted with a hearty laugh.

"No loss," he said, "these are for *his* funeral."

"Oh," said the girl, a smile overcoming her face, "that's good, I thought somebody had died."

"No, no, no," said the Death Coordinator, still laughing, still smiling.

"Not yet," added Cody, less of a smile on his face.

As she scanned the cards, the cashier said, "I always wondered what it would be like to plan my own funeral. I think about it every day. But it's always changing. Sometimes a customer brings up a card and I think to myself, I would love that at my funeral. And other times I think, I would hate that at my funeral. There are just so many things to consider. And you only get one funeral! It's the only thing in life that you only get one of. You can always get married again, graduate again, have another birthday party, another anniversary, go on another vacation. But you can't die a second time. You only get to die once. So, you want to make sure you die right. That you die in style. That means your funeral needs to be…"

As she continued to ramble, Cody watched the number on the screen climb higher and higher, moving into the next column and then the next. Growing a comma. Then moving, somehow, to yet another column.

She was still yammering about her dream funeral as Cody reached into his pocket and selected three credit cards to spread the charges.

After his total had been read to him in the same perky, happy voice that had moments ago greeted him, he handed over his cards and watched as she swiped his money away.

Before leaving, the Death Coordinator handed one final card to the girl.

"For when you're ready to plan your dream funeral," he said.

While Cody took Charlie for a short walk in search of a patch of grass for her to do her business on, the Death Coordinator returned to the car and made a note of all the purchases made inside.

He took the cards and inserted them in their prepared slots in his binder. He made a few calculations and looked at the estimated budget formed earlier in his office and made some quick adjustments. With Cody still not back, he pulled out his phone and scrolled through portfolios of prior clients. He found some with similar caskets, others with similar flower arrangements, and one that had the same combination of picture frame and wreath.

Cody opened the backdoor for Charlie and helped her to climb inside, then he took a seat beside her. Charlie immediately formed a donut shape and rested her head on Cody's lap.

"The budget is looking good," said the Death Coordinator. "I think you made some really great decisions in there."

Cody mumbled something about money and how little it mattered now.

* * *

The next few days were dedicated to the touring of local cemeteries. At each of the cemeteries, they were guided by a Plot Agent, who showed them every section of the cemetery which had plots available. Each of these Plot Agents spoke lovingly about their cemetery, telling Cody all of the things their cemetery had to offer that others didn't.

They were expert salespersons with pitches so well-rehearsed, so perfectly written, that Cody had to fight the urge to buy every plot offered.

"This is the cemetery every person hopes to one day be buried in. The souls here are happier than even the Souls up in Heaven. I mean it! They often say, 'No, thanks, God, I'm good right here. This cemetery is all I need.' It's true!"

And: "This area of the cemetery is typically reserved for people of extremely high regard: Presidents, national heroes, Nobel winners, star actors, and so on, but seeing that the Death Coordinator brings us so much business, I can probably get you in."

And: "While visiting your burial site, your loved ones will be able to sit by your graveside and watch as the ducks play in the lake across the way. And during the evening, the sun sets directly behind the lake and the view from this particular plot is absolutely breathtaking. And during the springtime, your spirit will be provided with unobstructed views of the cherry blossoms which add a level of beauty that other cemeteries have for decades attempted to emulate but cannot seem to master."

And so on and so forth.

But in the end, it wasn't Cody who chose his final resting spot. Nor was it any of the beautiful words from the Plot Agents.

Instead, Cody left his decision to Charlie.

For of the one hundred and sixty-two plots he was shown, there was only one plot that Charlie approached. She gently kicked the dirt around until it was warm enough, then she nestled herself atop the little piece of metal that marked the location of the plot.

Cody knelt down next to Charlie and petted her slowly.

"You like it here, Charlie?"

Charlie looked up at Cody with big, round eyes.

She didn't make a sound, but she did gently lick Cody's hand and wag her tail softly.

Cody looked up at the Death Coordinator and said, "This is the one."

"What a wonderful choice," said the Plot Agent beside the Death Coordinator. Cody had almost forgotten about him. "This is such a beautiful plot. Yes, it is! I will go write up the paperwork now."

The Plot Agent then climbed onto his golf cart and drove away, back to his office, leaving Cody and the Death Coordinator standing there, while Charlie quickly fell asleep.

Over the next couple of weeks, Cody, the Death Coordinator, and Charlie planned the rest of the funeral. They chose the venue, designed the tombstone, attended several tastings for the reception, and had Cody fitted for the suit in which he would be laid down for his eternal rest.

When all was said and done, and the entire list had been checked off, Cody had nothing left to do but wait for death to finally come and finish the job.

"Be careful in these final days," the Death Coordinator said to him after their final meeting. "Remember, debts and taxes cannot be evaded, not even in death. I have had many clients in the past whose husbands and wives, fathers and mothers, sons and daughters and forgotten cousins went wild on their final days, buying everything, going everywhere, burning through money that was never theirs to begin with. This sort of recklessness left my clients mourning the passing of their loved ones while also assuming responsibility for their newly formed debts. And I'm not sure which is worse for a person: the grief or the debt. After all, one fades with time, while

85

the other only accumulates."

With these words in mind, Cody spent his final days showing Charlie as much of the city as he could before he was gone. He took her to every park and beach and down every street. He wanted her to smell everything.

After all, the smells were free.

"Smell this," he said to Charlie.

And: "Smell this," he said.

And: "Come here, Charlie, you need to smell this."

It was on one of these walks, during one of these smelling tours of the city, that the cancer finally weakened Cody to his knees. He collapsed on the sidewalk and the leash with which he held Charlie in place dropped from his hand. But Charlie did not leave Cody's side. She stayed in place and barked at every passerby in sight, demanding that one of them—just one!—come to Cody's aide.

Yap! Yap! Yap! Yap! Yap!

But every person who walked by averted their eyes, each assuming that the next person would take an action they themselves refused. They each told themselves that if it had been another day, another situation, another time in which they weren't in such a rush, they would have been the one to stop, the one to call for help, the one to act.

Any other day.

But today—today, of all days!—they were so incredibly busy and they hadn't the time to stop and check on this fallen man and his barking dog.

It wasn't until the sun had set and Charlie had given up entirely on her barking and instead had rolled into a donut by Cody's side that an older lady, while on her way to the bus stop after a long shift at a nearby factory, finally knelt by Cody's side and felt for his pulse and realized that he was dead. She looked at Charlie who looked back at her and her eyes filled with tears, as did Charlie's. The lady wondered who to call first, 9-1-1, the city authorities in charge of keeping the streets clean of dead bodies, or Animal Services to come and take the dog.

In the end, she called the city, which sent a truck and a few workers to collect the body. In the left breast pocket of Cody's shirt, the workers found a business card for the Death Coordinator.

On the back it said—*If found, please call*.

And so they called.

"You have reached the Death Coordinator, where death is made just a little bit easier. How may I help you?"

The caller explained the situation.

"Is there a dog with the man?"

"There is."

"His name is Cody Wettenberg."

"The dog or the man?"

"The man. The dog's name is Charlie."

"Charlie," said the caller.

Charlie's eyes went up to the man, but her body did not move. She remained donut-like, nestled into Cody's cold body.

The Death Coordinator told the caller which mortuary had been paid in advance to take care of Cody's body.

"What about the—err—what about Charlie?" asked the man.

There was a silence.

"I'll be there momentarily to pick her up," said the Death Coordinator.

And then he hung up.

The next day, the Death Coordinator called everyone who needed to be contacted. And all the while, Charlie lay there by his side. The Death Coordinator had provided her with a bed, some bowls for water and food, a few toys, and several possessions of Cody's to keep his scent around for as long as possible.

Between incoming customers and phone calls, the Death Coordinator took Charlie on walks around the business complex. He had never really noticed the garden on site but it had quickly become

Charlie's favorite place to smell and the Death Coordinator's favorite place to sit and think. He had never really smelt the city before, but now he had learned to love it—along with the sounds: the cars, the planes, the nearby conversations.

And each day after work, on their way home, the Death Coordinator took Charlie to the cemetery Cody was buried in. There was no need to guide Charlie by leash. She knew exactly where to go.

As soon as he let her off the leash, she ran directly to the freshly laid dirt and, after a little digging to create herself a warm spot to lie down, she formed a donut in front of the tombstone, which read:

Here lies Cody Wettenberg.

Beneath his name were two prints:

One of Cody's left hand.

The other of Charlie's paw.

THE CRUMBLING

OF A NATION

AMERICA DID NOT COLLAPSE. IT crumbled. Nor did it crumble quickly. The crumbling occurred so slowly that no date could be attributed to the beginning of the end. Nor to the ending itself. It happened over decades, generations. The nation slowly fell alongside the pages of the calendar, the leaves from the trees.

It was a process as natural as the passing of time.

One flag was lowered, one office building was locked, one organization was shut down, one election was postponed, one courthouse was boarded up, one prison was overrun—and then another, and then another, until every flag had been lowered, every office had been locked, every organization had been shut down, every election had been indefinitely postponed, every courthouse had been boarded up, and every inmate had escaped.

And Francis Smith, the future heir of the Smith Empire, watched this crumbling occur through the floor-to-ceiling windows of his New York City penthouse, located on the 67th floor, which provided him with an unobstructed, panoramic view of Central Park.

It had been his favorite view as a kid. He loved to press his nose against the glass and stare at the people below. The park was always so alive. Some came to exercise, while others came to relax in the warm sun. Some came to talk with friends, while others came to get away.

But by the time Francis and his wife Eleanor and their three kids inherited the penthouse, along with the rest of the Smith Empire,

Central Park had become a symbol of America's decay. Every inch of the once beautiful park was covered with tents and wooden huts and broken-down trucks and rusty trailers and the men and women who called these decrepit things home.

Every tree had been cut down. Every statue had been covered in graffiti. The lakes had been turned into bathhouses. The museum had been overrun with squatters. The paintings had been burned for warmth and the statues within had been toppled and repurposed for shelter.

As the years came and went, the number of tents and people in the park continued to grow, as did the difficulties that Francis had convincing his children and grandchildren and great-grandchildren that Central Park really had been the most beautiful park in the world.

"You should have seen it! There were baseball games and friends throwing frisbees and people reading books and runners going every which way and children making angels in the snow and..."

But they did not believe him.

"No way," they said to him.

"That is not possible," they declared.

"You're making all that up," they accused.

And who could blame them?

The only Central Park they had ever known was filled with endless violence and gave off a stench so strong that it reached their noses sixty-seven floors above the ground.

How could it have ever been a beautiful place?

What was this crazy old man talking about?

"You'll see," Francis said to them. "One day, the park will be returned to its old glory. I know it! And then you'll know Central Park as I know it."

But not even he believed this. He knew Central Park was never going to be the same again.

And it made him sick.

After all, his ancestors had worked incredibly hard to purchase this penthouse on the 67th floor, and they had paid an exorbitant amount of money for it. One of the major reasons they were willing to spend so much of their hard-earned money to buy the penthouse was because of the beautiful view it provided of Central Park—and yet, in just a few short decades, the park, the view, and the value of the property itself had been entirely ruined.

Yes, oh, yes.

It made Francis sick.

But it wasn't only Central Park that had been ruined by the increasing number of New York City vagrants and rejects. And it wasn't only the value of his penthouse that they had lowered. It was every other aspect of the city, and every business in it, including the ones that had been handed down to Francis by his ancestors, from his factories to his investment groups, from his media companies to his prisons, from his hospitals to his construction companies, from his farms to his corporations—the entirety of the Smith Empire.

It was an epidemic that the city was unable to get under control. Nor the rest of the nation. These people overflowed into the streets, down alleyways, across bridges, and into every borough of New York City.

Everywhere Francis went, he was bombarded by beggars.

"Please, sir, please! Do you have any food?"

"Are you hiring? Sir, I am willing to do anything!"

"My son, sir, he needs some new shoes, do you happen to have a dollar you could spare."

Their tents were everywhere, entirely unavoidable, along with the violence that accompanied the culture of the impure and impoverished. Broken glass from smashed-up windows spread across sidewalks and glimmered beneath the ever-dimming streetlights overhead, as these good-for-nothings stole what they were incapable of earning on their own.

And many times, as a result of walking those dangerous streets,

Francis's shoes would get nicked or scratched and he would have to throw them away and replace them with new shoes fresh off the assembly line of his nearest factory.

"What are you looking at?" he'd say to a worker who happened to be nearby. "I am not paying you to stand around, am I?"

"No, sir."

"Then get back to work!"

"Yes, sir. I am on it, sir."

There was a constant state of fear in his workers' eyes—the fear that, if Francis was to let them go, they too would have no choice but to become one of the derelicts on the street.

Francis saw this fear. He could smell it. And he used it to drain every ounce of productivity from them. Many days he would just prowl the floors, the boardrooms, the cubicles, the hallways, letting his presence convey threats that need not be uttered.

After all, Francis Smith had an empire that he needed to keep in power. It was his family name stamped all over the New York City skyline. It was his name signed on the bottom of their weekly checks. It was his family that he fed with the money his companies made. And as he grew older, and as his family tree added new branches, he had to ensure that he had something great, something powerful to hand down to the next generation of Smiths .

He was the caregiver of the Smith Estate.

Like his father before him, and his father before him, and his father before…

As the number of tents in Central Park grew exponentially, so too did the violence, the unrest, the dangers of the city Francis had grown in, the city he had once loved. And before he knew it, the dangers had reached the doorstep of his empire. As the caregiver, he was faced with the difficult decision to remove his family, and his empire, from New York City. He gathered his three kids and eleven grandkids and over two dozen great-grandkids and the scores of in-laws and cousins and nephews and nieces he had accumulated over the years and ordered them all to pack their things.

"Don't ask questions," he said. "Just pack."

The decision forced upon him made him distraught. He mourned the city he had grown up in. He mourned the park he had spent his entire childhood adoring. He mourned the life that had been stripped from him by the good-for-nothings outside his window.

But as the caregiver of the Smith Empire, he had to prevent it from falling like every other great empire before it.

Like the American Empire was doing before his eyes, crumbling to dust.

And so, with a caravan that extended nearly a mile, the Smith family left New York City behind. But they did not travel alone. Francis knew, that for an empire to survive, workers were needed. So, before he shut the doors to each of his businesses, he recruited his top employees, the ones he knew would be able to contribute to his new society—construction workers and architects, doctors and nurses, chefs and bakers, security guards and artists. And they were glad to come, glad to escape the crime of New York City, glad to still have a job of any kind—glad to not be thrown to the streets like the thousands of former coworkers Francis had fired.

Their caravan was made up of car carriers, moving vans, bulldozers, forklifts, tractors, lumber trucks, livestock trailers, refrigerated trucks, tanker trucks, digger derricks, container lorries, and everything else needed for the Smith family to create a whole new world.

Guns peeked out the windows to deter thieves from approaching the caravan, though there were still thieves desperate enough to sacrifice anything—even their lives. As a result, many times their guns were shot, reloaded, and shot again.

The dead thieves were put to good use by their fellow peasants. Their pockets were picked, their clothes stripped, their limbs torn to pieces, their skin burned to a crisp, their bones carved into weapons, and their meat quickly digested by the savages who had recently considered them friends or family.

The workers saw this occur from the comfort of the vehicles provided to them by Francis and thanked the nearest Smith for saving them from such a harsh reality.

"Thank you, miss," they said.

"Thank you, sir," they said.

"Without your kindness, we would be just like them," they said.

"We owe you our lives."

The caravan traveled nearly two hundred miles northwest, to a large property that had been in the Smith Empire for over a century. The land was nothing more than crops and dirt for miles. But over a period of several months, the workers constructed for the Smith family a brand-new manor.

They built enough homes on the land for every Smith family, then quite a few more for future generations to come.

They scattered between the homes a few tennis courts, two golf courses, a couple basketball courts, a baseball diamond, a museum which stored the private collection of art that the Smith family had accumulated over the many generations, a library filled with tens of thousands of books once considered to be the rarest in the world (though now all books had become quite rare in America, as many bookstores and libraries had been burned in the pursuit of warmth), along with many other luxuries.

They dug numerous wells and ensured water was safely delivered to every home. They created sophisticated systems of sanitation and plumbing. They built a stable for the horses and a barn for the livestock and a pond for the soon-to-be sashimi.

They left behind several acreage of crops and planted gardens and anything else the Smith family needed to sustain life and, more importantly, enjoy the fruits of their ancestry.

As for the workers, Francis allowed them to remain on the property, though not within the walls they had built to protect his hard-earned sovereignty and the possessions of his inheritance. Instead, he graciously allowed them to build a settlement just beyond the manor walls. He kindly provided them, for just a few extra hours of work, all the leftovers from their travels and constructions. He gave them plenty of wood, shipping containers, vans, tarpaulin, rope, and everything else he was unable put to good use himself—or even half-decent.

With this material, the workers built themselves a settlement that somewhat resembled the lives of those who dwelled in Central Park, except this settlement was far away from the violent lives they would have been forced to live there.

And for this, they were grateful.

During the day, the settlers worked on the Smith Manor. They tended the crops, cooked the food, cared for the children, cleaned the houses, entertained the Smith family with music and theatre and art—in short, they served them in any way they were asked to do so.

At the end of each day, a dumpster filled with leftover food was rolled out into the settlement for them and their families to graze upon.

Occasionally, the dumpster was joined by a barrel of clean water.

Although the outside settlement had none of the luxuries that existed within the manor, the settlers were nonetheless exceedingly grateful for everything they were given. After all, they knew they had not earned any of it and that, without the kindness of the Smiths, who so willingly shared with them the accumulations of their generational efforts, they would have been left to fend for themselves like every other out-of-work vagrant in New York City —left to thieving for clothes and killing for crumbs.

But fortunately for the settlers, they had crossed the path of one of America's most gracious men—Francis Smith.

And for reasons they could not quite explain, Francis had chosen to save them, while thousands of their old coworkers were kicked onto the streets of New York City.

So, in honor of their savior, they named their settlement Francisville. And with the materials they accumulated over the next few years, they built near the entrance of the settlement a statue in his likeness.

But still, this felt to the settlers like an insufficient way of thanking Francis for all he had done for them.

And all he had saved them from.

Then one day, as a settler was cleaning Francis's home, he overhead Francis telling his great-grandchildren about Central Park.

"I would stand there for hours and watch the runners, the ball players, the readers, the sunbathers. It was the most beautiful place on Earth. But it is gone. It was stolen from our family. Your great-great-great-great-grandparents had earned us that view. And those—those peasants!—they took it away."

As the worker separated the food from the other bits of garbage in the trash, before transporting it to the dumpster, he came up with an idea.

Later that night, as he and his fellow settlers dug through the dumpster for their daily meal, he shared that idea with all of Francisville.

"Mr. Smith," he said as he picked the little bits of leftover chicken from the bone. "He loved Central Park as a kid. We can build him a new one, just outside his home. Then he can stand at his window and look out at it like he did as a kid."

They spent the rest of the night creating a blueprint of Central Park entirely from memory.

"No, the lake was there!"

"There were six softball fields, not five!"

"Don't forget the statue of that dog. Oh, what was his name? Ball —ball something—Ball…toe? Yes! Balto!"

They adjusted the locations of statues a few inches this way, a couple of feet that way. They argued over the size of the lake, the slopes of hills, the curvature of walkways.

Once they had finally agreed upon the location of every aspect of the park, they calculated the different ways to adjust the park's scale to fit the land in front of Francis Smith's home.

The following day, they began construction, trying to keep certain aspects secret—for instance, they covered the statues in tarpaulin, they did not form the softball fields until the project was near completion, the ponds were surrounded by wooden fences to prevent visibility, and any time they were asked what they were working on by a member of the Smith family, they would say that it was a 'top secret' order not to be revealed until it was ready.

It took them many months to complete the project. When it was done, all the settlers of Francisville gathered in front of Francis's house, along with the entire Smith family.

One of the settlers went to the door and knocked and, when Francis answered, said:

"Sir, we have something we would like you to see."

Francis, with the aid of his cane and a couple of servants, walked slowly outside.

"Move," he said to the settlers who blocked his way.

"Out of my way," he said.

And then, as he cleared the group and finally saw the park in front of him, a smile came over his face.

"Central Park," he whispered in his weakened and hoarse voice.

"It's just like I remember," he said.

"Kids! Kids! Look! It's just how I described."

Francis went inside his home and a few minutes later could be seen from the window on the third floor, looking out at the park.

He remembered everything.

Every afternoon he had spent with his nose against the glass.

He remembered the walkers and the joggers, the ball players and the frisbee throwers, the socialites and the isolationists, the sunbathers and the snow angel-makers.

And then he saw, in his mind's eye, the park—Central Park and the one in his manor—being overrun by tents and violent beggars.

He saw the walkers and joggers turn to sprinters who could not get away.

He saw the ball players and frisbee throwers lose their smiles, as their game turned deadly.

He saw the socialites split and the isolationists looking for anyone to help.

He saw the sunbathers covered in the shadows of invaders and the snow angels melting away.

He looked down and saw the settlers smiling up at him.

Waving.

And he felt sick.

THE TERMINATION

BUREAU

THE NURSES MOVED SYSTEMATICALLY THROUGH the incubator—giving bottles, changing diapers, checking charts, writing notes—when suddenly the doors swung open. All eyes turned to the man walking in. His stature cleared the doorway. His hair meticulously brushed to the side. Even his mustache had been combed to a tee. His uniform looked freshly pressed, down to the creases in his pants. The golden badge upon his chest glimmered in the light. A slim baton was tucked into his belt on his left; pepper spray on his right.

The nurses straightened, standing at attention.

"I need three more," he said to no one in particular.

One nurse quickly went into action, gathering three babies and their files onto her cart, and wheeling them eagerly to the officer.

"Here you go, sir," she said. "Three babies ready to go!"

She gave him a curtsy, brushing a few loose strands of hair behind her ear.

"Thank you, Miss Susan," said the officer with a wink.

Nurse Susan couldn't help but smile, her shoulders swaying from side to side.

"You're welcome, Officer Tommy," she said softly as he opened the door leading back to the room he had entered from.

The other nurses walked up to Nurse Susan's side.

"That man is such a hunk," said one.

"A real hero," said another.

Nurse Susan nodded, letting out a deep, wanting sigh as she did.

* * *

Against the back wall of the White Room stood twenty-six podiums. Like the walls, these podiums were painted daily with a fresh coat of white. But as the working day progressed, if one looked close enough, they would see several faint drippings of a red substance upon them.

Atop each podium was a tray about three feet in width, enclosed with thick, bullet-proof glass—though the front of the trays remained open. All had a baby on them.

Except for three.

Officer Tommy located these empty podiums and placed a baby atop their empty tray.

The collective sound of twenty-six babies crying was piercing. But Officer Tommy was used to it by then. He had worked in that particular office for several years and many more years in an office in Alabama, so he hardly even noticed the noise anymore.

Once he had confirmed that all the babies were securely on a tray, he collected their files from the cart and sat behind his desk on the opposite side of the room. He took his thermos of black coffee and had a small sip. The coffee was lukewarm, but he preferred it that way. It was a sign of a hard day's work.

He opened the file of the first baby and carefully looked over its information: a birth certificate, some information on the baby's birth parents, an application for termination, a couple of recommendations, an approval letter from the Moral Advisor, a signed Declaration of Release, the results from the baby's examinations, and so on.

Once satisfied, he moved on to the following file.

As Officer Tommy looked over the files, he could see the Waiting Room full of patients both young and old through the window on the eastern wall.

Each patient had their reason for being there that day, all rehearsing those reasons in their heads as they waited their turn.

Whenever the door to the Waiting Room opened, the room went immediately quiet, every whisper hushing. All eyes turned toward the door, at the secretary standing there, hoping their name would finally be called—wanting nothing more than to get this horrible, regretful day over with.

"Jocelyn Adams," said the secretary.

"That's me," a nervous voice said.

A thirteen-year-old girl stood. Her big, pregnant belly nearly knocked over the little kids playing in front of her. She stepped over a couple of babies as she made her way to the door.

"Excuse me," she said, "excuse me."

The secretary looked her up and down disgustedly as she watched this little kid approach her.

"Mmm," she said, "follow me."

And so Jocelyn Adams followed her to the back. The door closed and the Waiting Room once more filled with whispers—this time about the pregnant little girl.

Officer Tommy concluded that all the paperwork was in order. So he stood and made his way to the safes across the way, twelve in total, one for each Officer on staff. The safes were lined up just below the window looking into the Waiting Room.

For a moment, Officer Tommy studied the faces inside. The tears, the pain, the hopelessness, the nervousness—the shame. Then he waved with a smile.

But the patients did not wave back.

Still with a smile, Officer Tommy knelt before his personal safe, entered his combination into the padlock, and opened it carefully. He looked through every gun inside before choosing his favorite.

Then he filled his magazine with 26 bullets.

* * *

The secretary showed Jocelyn Adams to Office No. 3, where inside sat the Moral Advisor assigned her case. He was a tall man. A slender man. An old man. With a thick mustache as white as his skin.

"Sit," he said, without looking up. His voice was deep, commanding, and everything but welcoming.

Jocelyn sat in the chair across from him. She grabbed her application from her ripped-up backpack, setting it gently on the table. The application took all of the night prior to fill out. She had done so quietly, with her room lights off and only the light from her phone to guide her.

The Moral Advisor drew the papers closer to him. He placed a pair of half-moon reading glasses over his eyes.

Jocelyn tapped her toes anxiously as she watched him flip a page. She wiped sweat from her brow with her shirtsleeves. A minute later, he turned another page.

Her head started to pound. The fetus swayed inside.

A few pages later, the Moral Advisor stopped suddenly. He removed his reading glasses and looked up at Jocelyn.

"It seems," he said, "you have neglected to get the signature from the man who has impregnated you. According to the law here in the state of Florida, 'A pregnant girl or woman is not permitted to sell her baby without written permission from the man who impregnated her.' I am afraid I cannot approve your application."

"But sir," said Jocelyn, "you see…"

She stopped.

A tear rolled down her cheek. She averted her eyes from the Moral Advisor, whose judgment was piercing her skin.

She found a nice piece of carpet below to focus on instead.

"You see," she continued, "the man who impregnated me is… well… he… it was my father. And he refuses to sign."

The Moral Advisor grabbed the handbook from the shelf behind his desk. He flipped through the pages with familiarity. When he found the page he needed, he turned the book to Jocelyn and pointed at the seventh line on the left page.

As she looked at the words, the Moral Advisor rehearsed them from memory.

"It matters not who the man is—whether he be a blood relative, a rapist, a liberal, an atheist, a retard, or all of the above—if he is an American citizen, then it is his right to choose what becomes of his unborn child; the woman he impregnates is simply the carrier of his property, not the owner or decider of what happens to it."

Jocelyn looked up at the Moral Advisor stunned.

"Is your father an American citizen?" he asked her.

"He is," she said numbly.

"Well, in that case," said the Moral Advisor, taking his red stamp and slapping it on the front page of her application, "your application has hereby been denied by the state of Florida. And as the law requires for an impregnated woman, your baby must be carried to term and taken care of until the age of eighteen, or else, you will be sentenced to life in prison for the destruction or neglect of another man's property."

"But sir!" Jocelyn cried. "I cannot raise this child." The pounding in her head worsened. The fetus no longer swayed, but rocked.

"Then you should have thought about that before you went and got yourself pregnant, my dear," said the Moral Advisor, standing up from his chair.

"I didn't ask to get pregnant!" she screamed.

"Miss, I have other patients to see."

When Jocelyn refused to move, he grabbed her by her shoulders and shoved her out of his office, along with her backpack. Then he returned to his desk and pressed the button that called his secretary:

"Hold my next patient," he said. "I have to make a quick call."

Officer Tommy got into position in front of the first podium. He lifted the ocular lens to his right eye and ensured the baby's head was in sight.

According to the documentation, this particular baby had been placed into the care of the state of Florida by a married couple who attended the same church as Officer Tommy. In their application, they stated that, after many nights of prayer, it had been revealed to them that God had not willed this baby to be part of their family after all, and that God had told them it would be best to instead sell it to the state, so that it could go to wherever it was that God willed it to go.

The Moral Advisor assigned the case, someone who just so happened to believe in the same god as the patients believed in, approved this application almost instantaneously.

"God's will be done," the Moral Advisor wrote in the notes.

While the biological parents returned home after the birth of the baby, the baby remained in the hospital for several weeks, where the state of Florida ran multiple examinations to determine statistical likeliness that it would grow up to be a helpful servant of the state.

Every baby sold to the state went through these same tests. As a result of these tests, most were sent to various facilities around the state or sold to private organizations around the nation.

Those who tested high in intellectual potential were sent to academies that specialized in science, technology, and weaponry. The babies who tested high in muscular potential were sent to academies that specialized in physical labor. The babies testing high in loyalty and obedience were often sold to private organizations or the federal government for placement in the US military.

But every now and then, a baby failed to test high in any significant category and was determined statistically useless to the state, the federal government, and all private organizations.

This—the baby born to Officer Tommy's church-mates—just so happened to be one of those babies.

Officer Tommy blinked away the thoughts of his fellow churchgoers. Again, he focused on the baby across from him. He exhaled slowly, emptying his lungs, steadying his body, then held his breath as he pulled the trigger.

And just like that, the crying decreased by one.

* * *

In the alleyway behind the Termination Bureau, Jocelyn Adams grabbed the metal hanger that she had hidden before going inside. She had hoped she would not have needed to use it. She had hoped the Moral Advisor would have heard out her predicament, that her application would have been approved despite the missing signature. She had hoped...

But she had no more hope left to feel.

She had to use the hanger.

So she hid herself against the wall, in the shadows, away from the cameras, and carefully untwisted the hanger. She pulled the metal wire into a straight line.

She looked around one last time. No, there was nobody near and no cameras in sight to catch her.

She carefully took off her pants, followed by her underwear. All the while, leaning against the dumpster, she closed her eyes and inserted the wire inside herself in the same forceful way her father often entered her.

Even through the pain and discomfort, she continued to force the hanger deeper, just as she had seen in the videos she had studied the night before.

Tears poured down her cheeks as she scrambled the hanger to the left and right, up and down, side to side, until blood began to ooze out of her and onto her hand.

She dropped the hanger, falling to her knees.

The blood continued to flow.

She cried out in pain and guilt and sadness and hopelessness.

After all twenty-six targets inside the White Room had been terminated, Officer Tommy carefully disassembled his gun and returned it to his safe.

As he closed the door and locked the safe, he looked through the window into the Waiting Room.

They were no longer talking.

Just about all of the eyes were on the drops of blood behind him.

He smiled and waved, but received no response. He then turned back to his desk, grabbed twenty-six report forms from his filing cabinet, and filled them out one at a time.

Once all were completed, he placed the forms in their proper folders. He then tidied his desk—he stacked the folders, returned his pen to its holder, wiped away a smudge formed by his elbow, and took another sip of lukewarm coffee.

He then gathered the folders and took them to an adjacent room, where several desks were stationed.

He approached his secretary and set the folders gently on the table in front of her. He then leaned over and whispered something into her ear that only she could hear.

She blushed. She laughed. She bit her lower lip as she responded. And she did not push his encroaching hand away as it rubbed up and down her leg.

He then grabbed some water from a nearby cooler, checked in on a Moral Advisor friend of his, entered three dollars into the vending machine for a bag of chips and pocketed it for later.

Then he strolled back to the Incubator, whistling joyfully as he did.

"Nurses, I am ready for the next group."

It took no more than five minutes for police cars to fill the alleyway behind the Termination Bureau, for as soon as Jocelyn Adams left his office, the Moral Advisor called to let them know an act of murder was likely to be taking place in the alleyway. He told them to hurry, that there was still time to stop it, still time to save a life—though the life he was concerned for was only of the unborn; a life already started meant nothing to him.

Jocelyn had yet to pull up her pants by the time the police arrived.

She was just lying there in a pool of her own blood—crying.

The officers didn't bother to locate her missing pants. Instead, one police officer took her arms and roughly put them behind her back as his partner put his knees into her side.

"Stay down!" they yelled at her.

"Stay down!"

Another officer aimed his gun at her head, just in case she refused to listen.

He kept his finger on the trigger.

When she had been cuffed, they dragged her to the nearest car and threw her into the backseat, leaving behind a trail of blood.

With sirens playing in the background, Nurse Susan made her way around the Incubator as Officer Tommy watched her from the doorway to the White Room, which became less and less white as the day went on.

A BABY

IS BORN

A BUS PLASTERED IN ADS pulled up in front of the hospital. Three women emerged. The first was a few months pregnant. The second had a feeling she just might be. And the third was already very much in labor.

It was this woman who was quickly swarmed by a group of men and women all yelling at once:

"Maybelline! Maybelline!"

"Have you signed up with a cereal brand yet?"

"Have you chosen your child's favorite sports teams?"

"Do you know what religion you are going to raise your baby in?"

"What T-shirts are they going to wear?"

"Can I tell you about our incredibly comfortable socks?"

"Maybelline! Over here! Over here! Have you heard about the shows ABC is planning to produce in the coming decade?"

On and on, these Recruiters screamed at Maybelline, trying desperately to get her to agree to a lifelong contract with their company on behalf of her unborn child in exchange for a hefty check before she had even entered the hospital, wherein they would then need to pay the hospital itself for access to her.

They were relentless—standing between her and the door, doing everything they could to prevent her from going inside.

Nor was this the first time they had harassed her.

They had been soliciting her since the moment her pregnancy test came back positive and the results were sent from the Baby Birthing Hospital to all of the companies in the area, and then—after the two-week legally mandated waiting period—every other company in this great nation. Which only intensified the soliciting, the harassment, the letters, the targeted commercials, the billboards in front of her apartment complex.

They called her at all hours of the day and night. They came into her office in the middle of the workday and slipped her boss a twenty for the keys to her cubicle, which was only permitted to be unlocked during her thirty-minute lunchtime and her pre-approved bathroom breaks.

And when she locked herself in her apartment, the Recruiters still came—her landlord's pocket getting fatter night after night.

So, unsurprisingly, by the time the bus dropped her off in front of the hospital, she was sick and tired of all the offers, all the Recruiters, all the questions.

And yet, they kept coming.

Even as she reached the front desk.

There were advertisements all around it, covering the wall and the desk itself—billboards and brochures, stickers and water bottles, business cards and flyers, all covered in slogans and promises and offers.

Even the man behind the desk was covered in ads.

"Hello, miss," he said. "Who is sponsoring your visit today?"

Maybelline told him that her hospital entrance fee was to be sponsored by three corporations in exchange for her child's lifelong patronage. She handed him contracts signed in both ink and blood, along with the checks and patches the corporations provided for her baby's suit.

"Wonderful choices," said the man. "These are some great corporations. Especially this one."

As he said this, he pointed at his right shoulder where stitched into his clothing was the very same patch. "They are one of the best companies in America. Don't you agree?"

But Maybelline was unable to respond, for a contraction had come just as she opened her mouth to do so.

Instead, she let out a scream.

"Ahhhhhhhhhhhhhh!"

"Oh, boy," said the man behind the desk. "Let's get you into a room, shall we?"

The advertisements continued in her hospital room, where a nurse gave her a hospital gown to change into.

It too was covered in advertisements.

When the nurse left the room, Maybelline slid out of her bodysuit which was covered in the many patches she had acquired throughout her life—some given to her at birth, a few more provided whenever a corporation sponsored one of her childhood activities, and many more given to her whenever she took out a loan of any sort— and dressed in the gown provided.

She then lay in bed and stretched out her legs. The television across the room played pitches from various brands and their Recruiters. She closed her eyes and tried to ignore them. But the volume had been turned up as loud as the TV would allow, and she could not avoid their messages.

She sat up in bed and looked around the room for a remote control but could not find one. She got out of bed and walked up to the television, only to discover that all the buttons had been removed. Nor could she unplug it, for all the wires had been glued into place.

Seeing no other option, Maybelline returned to bed, closed her eyes, plugged her ears with her fingers, and waited for the doctor to come and take this damn baby out of her.

But the doctor was not the first to enter the room.

Instead, Maybelline had to entertain several visitors before she could be permitted to see the doctor. In total, 28 Recruiters (representing companies that sold things like TVs, video games, shoes, trading cards, furniture, magazines, newspaper subscriptions, streaming services, sporting equipment, plants for future gardens, etc. etc.) entered the room.

"Think about it," said the Recruiter from the television company. "Your kid will spend most of their life staring at a screen. Don't you want them to be staring at the best of the best? Don't you want the colors to pop? Don't you want every pixel to be beautiful? Don't you want the sound to fully engulf them? Don't you want their life to be filled with beautiful images? Don't you want…"

And: "Remember," said the Recruiter from the furniture store, "the discounts offered to your child today become active as soon as the contract is signed. Your baby may not yet need a recliner in the living room, but I bet somebody you know would love one. Hmm? Is it true what I read in your files? You and your husband each work 90+ hours a week, yet you still have to take out loans to pay your bills? Is that why he isn't here today? Is he unable to afford even just one day off to watch his baby be born? Boy…he must be exhausted. He must just love relaxing at home, putting his feet up, and having support during those few hours a week of leisure time. If only you could get him—I don't know—an incredibly comfortable recliner chair at a slightly discounted price. I wonder if there is any way you could do something like…"

And: "If you sign this contract today," said the Recruiter from a nationwide nursery, "declaring your child will buy all their future plants, trees, seeds, pots, and so on from us, we are not only willing to give them 10% off all of our products for life, but we will also pay 7% of your total hospital bill today and up to 3% of future hospital bills throughout your child's life, as long as they remain loyal to the agreement made on their behalf today. As long as they…"

Similar conversations were had with each of the Recruiters.

And as they left, each gave the same ultimatum:

"You have until the time your baby is born to decide. After that, this deal is off the table. And remember: the hospital bill is due before your baby can leave. Otherwise, the child becomes property of the highest bidder. I'd hate to see you leave here without your baby. That would be quite a shame."

"How are you feeling?" asked the doctor when she finally entered the room at the conclusion of the 28th meeting, nearly four hours after Maybelline's arrival at the hospital.

She responded with a detailed analysis of what each of her body parts was feeling.

"My back feels like it is about to split. My knees are pounding faster than my heart. My skin is on the verge of tearing. My arms are—"

But the doctor cut her off.

"No, no, no," said the doctor, laughing. "I meant about the presentations. How are you feeling? Pretty good, weren't they?"

On the lapel of the doctor's coat were patches identifying her credentials. There was one from the university where she had earned her doctorate, one from the company that owned the hospital, and one from each board she was currently a member of.

Scattered over the rest of her coat were patches of various-sized advertisements.

"Obviously," the doctor went on to say, gesturing at those patches, "I have been monetarily influenced to persuade you in a particular direction."

Maybelline nodded.

"My employers would like me to sit here and say, 'Sign up for this brand,' and 'This particular religion will teach your child the best morals, while this religion will send your child straight to hell,' and 'This organization has a terrible reputation, while this one has always been reliable and loyal to its customers.' They provide me with scripts, presentation materials, and hefty checks whenever I am successful. You know how these companies are—only ever thinking about money, money, money."

Maybelline and the doctor laughed together. They both knew the lengths corporations would go for seventy, eighty, ninety years of business from a single customer. They had been shown the math in grade school. They were reminded of it daily. They knew that, even after giving tens of thousands of dollars away, these companies always made their money back in the end.

And then some.

According to numerous studies, the number of years needed for a corporation to break even on their investment, depending on the size of the loan and the offered discount, was roughly thirteen years.

After that, it was nothing but profit.

So, the more years a company had exclusive rights to a customer, the more profit they could make.

Hence, the presence of Recruiters now outside every Baby Birthing Hospital in America, all now in the hands of private organizations specializing in the selling of contracts to newborn babies through loans given to parents to cover the price of giving birth inside their hospital.

Nor could parents opt to birth elsewhere, after years of lobbying had made them the only legal place to give birth in America. And the only way to leave a Baby Birthing Hospital with your baby in hand was to pay the bill on the day of birth.

"Anyway," said the doctor, pulling a clicker out of her pocket and pointing it at the television screen, changing the channel to a presentation, "if you direct your attention to the screen, I will show you just how much your child's life will be improved if you agree to make the Pepsi Bottling Group their beverage company of choice."

After concluding her presentation, the doctor turned to leave the room. "I will give you a few minutes to think things over," she said on her way out, leaving behind a screaming, sweating, pain-filled Maybelline. One who still had lots of decisions to make before she could even think about pushing this baby out.

After a few minutes had passed, an Unbiased Mediator entered the room. Every Baby Birthing Hospital in America was required by law to have an Unbiased Mediator on its staff. It was their job to ensure no funny business took place during the signing of contracts and the passing of checks. The Unbiased Mediator who entered the room was a man in his late sixties, although he had undergone many procedures to disguise this fact. The procedures had been so successful that he presented as a thirty-year-old man who had never worked a day in his life—unlike Maybelline, who, at the age of thirty-seven, looked on the verge of seventy. The Unbiased Mediator's wrinkles had been entirely eradicated, his hair had been dyed jet black and groomed in a way that made the thinning unnoticeable, his lips had been filled with synthetic hyaluronic acid, his nose had been surgically reshaped, and the sclera of his eyes had been repeatedly dyed white, along with his teeth. He wore a perfectly tailored suit, which was navy blue and covered in patches from various corporations.

"Hello…Maybelline, is it?" he said upon entering, checking his notes as he closed the door behind him. "What an exciting day this must be for you."

"Yes," said Maybelline, "my husband and I are very excited to bring home our first child."

This, of course, was not what he was referring to. And she knew it. And he knew that she knew it. And she knew that he knew that she knew it.

And so on.

"Before we begin the paperwork," said the Unbiased Mediator, "I was wondering if you wouldn't mind one final presentation?"

Maybelline knew this question was nothing more than rhetorical and that only one answer would suffice. So, she gave it.

"Oh, boy, another presentation? Please, please! I would love another!"

"Wonderful," said the Unbiased Mediator with a smile. Out of his Gucci briefcase, he pulled a remote that was covered in diamonds.

He pointed it at the screen and began his presentation.

Over the next hour, he told Maybelline, in incredible detail, about his favorite corporations, offering her many incentives if she signed up with them—incentives he too would benefit from. And not only did he mention his favorite corporations, but he also made sure to include the corporations he highly discouraged her child from affiliating with, all of which just so happened to be in direct competition with his affiliations.

Finished with the presentation, the Unbiased Mediator returned his diamond-studded remote to his Gucci briefcase and exchanged it for a stack of papers, along with a luxury fountain pen that was gold-plated and also covered in diamonds.

"Now," he said, resting the stack on his lap, "have you decided which corporations you would like your child to be affiliated with?"

Before she could respond, Maybelline felt another contraction coming.

"Ahhhhhhhhhhhhhh—yes," she said through gritted teeth. "I have made up my mind."

"Wonderful," said the Unbiased Mediator, still smiling. He looked down at the papers in his lap and asked the next question. "Have you in any way felt unfairly or inappropriately pressured to sign your child up with any particular corporation today?"

Maybelline laughed at the question.

"Of course not," she said. "All is fair in the pursuit of money. Is it not?"

The Unbiased Mediator did not respond to her question. Instead, he continued to read from the script provided to him by the United States Congress.

"Before you provide me with the corporations, please keep in mind that these affiliations are binding and will remain so throughout the life of your child. If they, meaning your child, renege on any of these affiliations, they—and you, the caregiver who signed the contract on their behalf—will be heavily fined and thrown into prison for a minimum of five years per infraction. With that being said, are you ready to proceed?"

Maybelline had no choice. She knew that she could not afford the bill. She knew she could not live with the decision to sell yet another child to the highest bidder. She knew her remaining years of fertility were winding down. She knew all she and her husband had ever wanted was to start a family.

She knew what needed to be done.

She knew what she needed to say.

So, she said it.

"Yes, I am ready to proceed."

In the end, she affiliated her unborn child with 48 corporations who collectively assumed all costs of her child's birth which, by the end of the day, amounted to well over two million dollars.

The Unbiased Mediator ensured every line was signed, every 'i' dotted, and every 't' was crossed before leaving the room.

"You have made some wonderful decisions today," he said to Maybelline on his way out.

Once outside, he looked at the doctor who patiently waited in the hall and said, "Every dollar has been accounted for. Miss Maybelline is ready to give birth."

The Unbiased Mediator handed the clipboard filled with contracts to the doctor.

"Wonderful job, my friend," said the doctor, reviewing the decisions made by Maybelline. "Wonderful job, indeed."

The doctor entered the room just as another contraction hit.

"Ahhhhhhhhhhhhh!"

"Well," said the doctor with a little laugh, "it sounds like that baby is ready to come out, doesn't it?"

The doctor put on her gloves, adding, "By the way, I saw the list of corporations you signed up with. It is a very impressive list. Your child is going to be very happy when it grows up. They are going to live such a wonderful life—I just know it."

"Ahhhhhhhhhhhhh!" was Maybelline's response.

"Yes, yes. A wonderful life, indeed," said the doctor, placing herself between Maybelline's legs for the first time all day.

"Now," she said, "let's have ourselves a look, shall we?"

Maybelline did not have the chance to hold her newborn baby before she was taken out of the room for a thorough evaluation. All she saw was her baby in the hands of the doctor while the umbilical cord was snipped by the highest bidder.

The placenta was handed to another.

"Can I hold her?" Maybelline asked the doctor. "Please!" she cried, "let me hold my baby!"

"Not yet," said the doctor in response, "her sponsors want her immediately evaluated. After all, they are paying quite a lot for her today. And they want to ensure their investment is worth it while they still have time to void their contract."

Once her sponsors were satisfied, the baby was brought back to Maybelline.

While she was gone, she had been cleaned and dressed in a onesie covered in the patches of her new affiliations.

Maybelline eagerly took the baby in her arms and swayed her gently back and forth.

"The corporation that paid for the rights is currently deliberating over her name," said the doctor. "I will inform you when that decision has been made. Until then, try to get some rest."

And with that, the doctor left the room.

Immediately upon the closing of the door, Maybelline began to cry, entirely overwhelmed by a flood of emotions.

At first, she was overcome with joy at the arrival of her child.

Then that joy became anxiety about the world she was to raise that child in.

Then came pity.

Then anger.

Then guilt.

Then hopelessness.

As the emotions continued to evolve, the tears continued to fall down the cheeks of Maybelline and her baby, not yet named.

LOVE, THE WAY

GOD INTENDED

THE ADMINISTRATORS OF WASHINGTON MIDDLE School could no longer sit idly by as the dangers of the outside world crept into their community, threatening their students—in heart and in mind and in body. Too many events had already occurred around the nation—the librarian in Oregon with the rainbow flag on her desk, the bus driver in New York who played gangster rap over the radio every morning, the group of sixteen-year-olds in Ohio with watermelon charms on their Crocs.

They had seen too much to turn a blind eye.

They had to be proactive.

So they installed security procedures that rivaled any other in the nation. All who stepped foot on their campus first had to go through a multi-tiered security system—teachers, students, parents, administrators. Even the mailman was subject to this high level of security.

And security only increased once inside.

Teams of police officers and retired soldiers with constantly loaded guns on their hips monitored the hallways. Cameras were installed inside every classroom, down every hall, throughout the playground, on the gates that surrounded the campus, and anywhere else a potential danger could possibly be. All potential employees had to go through intense background checks and psychiatric tests before they were even given the chance to interview for a job so near the youth of this great community.

The school had to protect their kids.

* * *

Mrs. Estrada was the seventh-grade English teacher at Washington Middle School. But she had never wanted to be a teacher. After watching Michael Phelps win yet another gold medal as a kid, she wanted to be an Olympic swimmer. She had once considered becoming an astronaut or a veterinarian or maybe a fashion designer. For two years in high school, she thought going to the WNBA was a real possibility. And at one point in college, sitting in the library at two in the morning, she thought life would have been a heck of lot easier if she had just become a stripper.

But in the end, following in the footsteps of her mother and father and all the other men and women she knew with a medical degree, she became a doctor.

In particular, she became a pediatrician. And she was good at it. She did it for many years. But watching what was happening around the nation, and hearing from her patients about the changes taking place in her local schools, she felt a sudden call to change her profession to education. She had heard her community's cry to protect their kids. And that's what she wanted to do—protect the kids. So she sent in her application, underwent the required psychiatric evaluations, the intensive interview process, the years of additional schooling and training, and was now well into her sixth year as a seventh-grade English teacher at Washington Middle School.

She joined the back of the line for security, which was already wrapped around the corner even though school wasn't set to begin for another forty-five minutes. Everyone in line waited patiently. Like her, they were used to these intricate, laborious security procedures. And many agreed this was necessary for their kids' safety.

As she waited, she altered the arm carrying her box of books, occasionally setting the box down to rest her arms entirely. When her turn finally came, she set the box on the conveyor belt, removed her shoes, belt, jewelry, and electronics, then walked through the body scanner.

"Clear," said the first security guard, and onward she walked, to a second security guard who scanned her once more with a wand, just in case the body scanner missed anything.

"Clear," said the second security guard.

The box of books and the rest of her belongings were also scanned while a third security guard observed. Once the box had reached the other side, yet another security guard grabbed the top book, eyeing it.

"These books received approval?" he asked.

"Yes, sir." Mrs. Estrada pulled the signed paperwork from her pocket and handed it over. The security guard looked through the paperwork, checking the legitimacy of the signatures from the school board, principal, and state governor. He then compared the title on the paperwork with the top row of books. Everything matched. He handed the paperwork back to Mrs. Estrada, though his evaluation was far from complete, and picked up a copy from the top row, reading the title of the book and its author out loud, along with the description on the back of the book. Nodding approvingly, he removed the dust jacket and studied the boards, then carefully scanned the pages within to ensure they all matched the description he had just read. Again, he nodded approvingly. Lastly, he went through the box, ensuring every cover matched those on the top of the box.

Finally satisfied, the final security guard said, "Clear."

When Mrs. Estrada got into her classroom, she kept the door locked, the blinds drawn, and the lights off. Relying on feel and faint outlines, she made her way to the back table, where she gently set down the box of books. Carefully, she removed each book and set them down in front of her.

Each book had upon it a picture of a young boy and a young girl holding hands. Written in big, bold letters was the title of the book: *Love, the Way God Intended*.

A raving review from the nation's most popular news organization called the book, "A triumph for American society and future generations."

The story follows the lives of two elementary students who later married and started a family. They came from great, wealthy, religious households that blessed them with wonderful morals no other child around them seemed to have. And every time they found themselves tempted to behave like those around them, they needed only to hold their lover's hand and remember the morality placed in their hearts by their parents and their God. It was a beautiful telling of how God could defeat the evilness of humanity, a beautiful telling of how love could triumph evil, and a beautiful telling of what morality truly looked like.

As Mrs. Estrada arranged the books on the desks around the class, one dust jacket slipped to reveal that underneath it was not actually a copy of *Love, the Way God Intended*, but rather a book called *We Do Not All Love the Same, and That's Okay*—a book that had been banned by her school district and many other districts and libraries throughout the state and nation for its inappropriate inclusion of same-sex relationships and drag queens and polygamy and other methods of love that did not align with the views of many.

Mrs. Estrada quickly readjusted the jacket to ensure the book appeared like the others.

She looked around nervously, at the cameras around her classroom, at the little cracks in the window, then hurried to her desk to grab some tape.

As she finished taping the dust jacket to the book, the bell suddenly rang.

Frantically, she opened the blinds, turned on the lights, returned the tape to her desk, and unlocked the door.

She forced a smile as she welcomed the class with her usual:

"Good morning and God bless."

* * *

After the morning prayers had been spoken over the loudspeaker, Mrs. Estrada introduced the class to their new book by reading from the script provided to her by the school board.

"*Love, the Way God Intended*," she read, "is a monumental novel taking the nation by storm for the morality it strives to return to American households. This story serves as a much-needed blueprint for how love and relationships should look in a society too often deceived by the Devil and his advocates. It is the sort of book that has the potential to wipe away millions of sinful acts before they even occur, the type of book that can change the actions of an entire society, the type of book that comes at the perfect time, delivering the perfect story. It is the book this nation needs to save itself from the…"

The script went on for several more minutes. Afterwards, she led the class in a short discussion about what they thought love should look like and how it should feel and whom that love should be between. She then assigned them a worksheet to help them reflect on that discussion. As they worked on the worksheet, she walked around the class, making sure all of their answers corresponded with the answer sheet the school board provided her. After collecting the worksheets, she ordered them to open their books to page seven, where the prologue began.

Once everyone had made it to the proper page, she began reading, and they all followed along—except for a certain four who found within not a copy of *Love, the Way God Intended*, like the dust jacket and Mrs. Estrada's instruction implied, but rather an entirely different book: *We Do Not All Love the Same, and That's Okay*. This was not the first time these four students had been assigned a book unlike the others, so they were not surprised to find that their books began on a completely different page and included words that did not match what Mrs. Estrada read aloud to the rest of their classmates.

These students, like their books, were not like the others. They had souls that had been banned from the state where their bodies dwelled. Nor did their souls align with the world propagandized in the book that the school board demanded Mrs. Estrada read. In the simplest terms, they did not love in the way God intended. They did not present themselves to the world in the way their politicians preferred. They did not—

The doors to the classroom opened, and in walked three police officers.

"Random search," one of them declared as another stepped up to the nearest student's desk, grabbed their backpack, and dumped out their belongings. The three officers searched through the dumped-out items, finding a pencil box, a notebook, a binder, a textbook, and a lunch pail. One officer sifted through each item in the pencil box. Another carefully investigated every word written on the pages of the notebook, while the third did the same with the contents of the binder.

Once every item had been evaluated, the officers dropped everything back on the desk.

"Clear," said one of the officers.

Onward they moved, on to the next student, where again the officer dumped out everything within their backpack: a loose pencil, a notebook, a pocketknife, a sandwich in a plastic bag, a handheld video game console, and even a handgun. The officers crowded around the table again. One lifted the gun and found it to be loaded. He rolled the bullets around in his hand before slotting them back inside the gun, then placed it back among the items. Another officer picked up the pocketknife and ejected each of the tools—several of them seemed to have been freshly sharpened. One of them even cut the officer as he fiddled around with it.

Then:

"Clear," said one of the officers.

They moved on to the next student, repeating the process over again, ensuring no illegal paraphernalia existed anywhere among

LOVE, THE WAY GOD INTENDED

the items. They cleared this student, then moved on to the next.

Another half dozen students later, the officers approached the first student who had on their desk a false copy of *Love, the Way God Intended*. The officers grabbed this student's backpack, dumping their belongings on the desk.

Among the mess was the hidden copy of *We Do Not All Love the Same, and That's Okay*.

One officer picked up a notebook and looked at the content inside.

"Whose initials are these?"

The student panicked, knowing the initials did not belong to a person of the proper sex. Fortunately, several students at the school shared those initials, many of whom were of the proper sex, so the student randomly selected one and provided their name to the officer.

Satisfied, the officer dropped the notebook to the desk.

"Clear."

All the while, Mrs. Estrada continued reading from the book and the students followed along, even as the officers prowled around the room. Mrs. Estrada's voice was shaky, and she often stumbled over her words, though she relaxed slightly as the officers cleared two more of the students she had provided with illegal reading material.

When the officers poured out the backpack of the final student whose book differed from the others, the book itself was knocked to the floor along with a few other items. As the student reached for the book, one officer stopped them. He then picked the book up himself, turning it over slowly. It was the same officer who had cleared Mrs. Estrada when she entered the school earlier that morning.

His eyes fixated on a little strip of tape. He did not remember this from his earlier evaluation, or with any of the other books. He asked a nearby student for their pocketknife.

Mrs. Estrada stopped reading.

She could not move. She could not think.

Everyone was watching now as the officer cut the tape. He returned the pocketknife to the student and removed the dust jacket from the book, revealing behind it *We Do Not All Love the Same, and That's Okay.*

All three officers drew their guns and aimed them at the student.

"Get down on the ground!"

"Put your hands on your head!"

The third officer turned his gun on Mrs. Estrada.

"Did you know about this?"

He raised the book in the air.

"No, sir," she said. "You saw the books yourself this morning. They were all correct. I would never allow that sort of—that sort of *filth* in my classroom."

The officer nodded, then turned to the student on the floor. He pressed his knee into their back.

"Do not resist! I said, Do not resist!"

Aggressively, he cuffed the student's hands behind their back.

And as quickly as the officers had barged in, they left, now dragging the student behind them.

The class was visibly disturbed—not so much from the treatment of their fellow classmate, but rather from the idea that such a book had been in their presence all this time. They carefully studied their books, ensuring none of those words had somehow managed to jump into theirs. Comforted by their discoveries, they returned their attention to their spilled-out belongings.

"Take the next few minutes to clean up your belongings," said Mrs. Estrada. "We will resume reading in three minutes."

As the students slowly cleaned their belongings—their pencils, their binders, their notebooks, their guns, their lunch pails, their pocketknives, their textbooks, their electronics—and returned them to their backpack, Mrs. Estrada hid behind her desk.

Tears poured from her silently.

She could not let the students hear her, nor the cameras overhead see.

Beneath her desk, visible only from her crouching position, were several tallies scratched into the wood. Mrs. Estrada took a pocketknife from her own pocket and extended one of the blades. Quietly, she etched one more tally into the wood alongside the rest—now twelve in total—and took a moment to mourn the ones she had been unable to save. Then she thought of the others—the ones she had saved, at least if only for a moment. The ones she had been able to introduce to ideas the state had forbidden.

She remembered why she made the switch to education in the first place:

To protect the kids.

Or, at least, the ones she could.

Once she had regained her composure enough to continue, she stood and grabbed her copy of *Love, the Way God Intended*.

"Okay, class," she said, her voice slightly shaking, "what page were we on, again?"

"Fifteen," called one student.

"That's right," said Mrs. Estrada. "Please turn back to page fifteen."

Everyone returned to page fifteen.

Except for three, who still had their copies of *We Do Not All Love the Same, and That's Okay* opened in front of them.

WE SEE

YOU

HER FINGER HOVERED OVER THE touchpad of her laptop. The pointer on the screen hovered over the submit button. Her future hovered over her, filling the library.

She had dedicated every second of the past four years to this thesis and with just the slightest movement of her finger it would all be over. She wondered if she had put in enough time, if the sources were scholarly enough, if the data was conclusive enough, if the research was thorough enough, if she had worded everything just right, if she had overlooked some egregious misspelling or grammatical error, if she had cited everything exactly as her professor expected, if she had effectively rebutted every counterargument presented.

The voices in her mind screamed and her heart pounded and the last four years flashed before her eyes and the infinite paths of her future stretched and then shrunk. She saw herself thirty years down the line—a sad, pathetic disappointment, mumbling on the streets about a thesis that...

She pressed submit.

And, just like that, her mind quieted and the visions dissipated and a pop-up box appeared on the screen confirming the receipt of her submission, along with a short congratulatory message:

> *Congratulations, Anna Lee!*
> *Your thesis has been successfully submitted! A con-*

firmation email has been sent to your university email address. Please check your email for further details.

The title of Anna Lee's thesis was *The Lifelong Criminal: How the Justice System in America Fails to Rehabilitate, Restore, and Revive the Life of its Inmates*. Restorative justice has been a deeply personal topic to Anna Lee ever since her brother fell victim to the system many years ago.

He was a good kid who happened to be in the wrong place at the wrong time. He was with the wrong crew. He was uninvolved in the acts committed, and yet the jury found him complicit by association.

As a result, he was sentenced to six months in prison.

Those six months were all it took to ruin his future.

He came home a different person—someone Anna Lee did not recognize. And when he drunkenly attacked their mother, Anna Lee knew this person was not her brother. It was somebody else—a monster that had latched upon her brother in that horrible place called prison.

He had not been rehabilitated. He had been poisoned. Tainted. Forever changed and ruined.

Anna Lee still visited him every Saturday afternoon in the prison where he was sentenced to remain for twenty-two more years. And every now and then, during these visits, she would catch a glimpse of her former brother hidden behind the darkness of his new eyes.

In these times, she grabbed his hands and promised she would not allow the system to take any more brothers from their sisters.

She wrote all about him in her thesis. All about the life he could have lived, the life that was stolen from him because he happened to be in the wrong place on the wrong night, and as a result was locked away in a place no human should ever be—not even the worse of them. Not even the most depraved.

Anna Lee believed in second chances.

But she had spent enough time and energy in the stolen world of her brother to know second chances, though promised, were not provided by this nation.

As she exited the library, she attempted to wipe away the thoughts of prison, her brother, and the other bits and pieces of her thesis.

After all, tonight was a night of celebration. After ten long years —four years of undergrad and two years in her masters program and four more years in her doctorate program—her thesis was finally finished, her schooling was complete. And downtown, in a bar she planned to get extremely wasted in, a group of her closest friends were awaiting her arrival.

So, she put in her headphones and blasted a playlist she had made just for this occasion, and waited as the thoughts of her thesis slowly faded away.

And as she danced through campus, she texted her friends:

"I'm on my way! Get the tequila going!"

Every hundred or so feet, Anna Lee passed by poles with blue lights repeatedly flashing at their tops. Each of these poles had emergency phones attached to them which connected directly to the local police. They had been installed on campus many years ago in hopes of preventing emergencies of all kinds—mostly violent and sexual acts committed on female students and staff.

Though Anna Lee had always thought the blue lights served less as a preventative and more as a reminder of the reality women like herself had long been forced to accept. A reality that seemed to say:

We can't protect you, but hey—*we see you.*

Anna Lee tried not to let these blue lights dampen her mood but this deliberate suppression of reality, like suppressing the reality of the harm done to her brother by America's *in*justice system, only brewed more guilt within. It felt like trying to smile through the rapes that were never prevented—nor punished—and hardly acknowledged except with a few blue lights on campus.

But what other choice did she have? If she dwelled on the lights, if she let them bring her down, then the men who made the lights necessary in the first place would win.

So she had to smile. She had to carry on.

She had to.

And so she did. She danced through campus and continued to dance as she made her way through the downtown streets, en route to the bar and her friends and many, many tequila shots. She lip-synced along with the words blasting in her ears. She skipped over the cracks in the path she followed. She twirled. She hopped. She skipped. She—

She hit the floor.

It started with a whistle that Anna Lee did not hear from a man she did not see. He was sitting, leaning against the wall of a boarded-up building, smoking a cigarette, drunkenly slurring.

"Hey, beautiful," he said to Anna Lee.

But she did not hear him.

"Can I dance with you, hot stuff?" he said a little louder, smiling uncontrollably, standing and nearly falling over.

"Don't ignore me, baby doll," he said to Anna Lee who continued to dance, unfazed and unbothered.

"I just want to talk," he howled.

"Hey, bitch!"

He tossed his cigarette to the side and stood fully erect for the first time.

"I am talking to you."

But Anna Lee ignored him. Or so it seemed to him. And he refused to be ignored.

Taking his first step toward Anna Lee, he yelled, "Where the fuck do you think you're going?"

Anger filled his eyes as the first camera was aimed in his direction. The holder of the camera was a fourteen-year-old boy eating ice cream with his friends across the street. He licked the top scoop of rocky road and nudged his friends with his elbow.

"Look," he said.

And so they looked, each drawing phones of their own as they did, as the man continued to approach Anna Lee, yelling out horrible things with each step.

Like: "Stop dancing, you bitch!"

And: "I said, Do not walk away from me!"

And: "Listen, Baby, I just want to talk!"

And: "Slow the fuck down!"

By the time he reached Anna Lee and threw her to the ground, sixteen cameras were filming his every move. He ripped the headphones from her ears before she could even react. And by the time she turned to face her attacker, she was slapped.

17 cameras—18, 19, 20; 25, 30, 35.

"You think you're too good for me, don't you, bitch?"

Anna Lee tried to yell for help. She tried to yell at him. She tried to yell. She tried to make a sound. But she couldn't. She was frozen. She could not move her lips. Her tongue was immobile. Her voice had been swallowed, hidden in a place she could no longer find.

The man stood over her.

"You women," he said. "You women are always ignoring men like me. Don't you know that we have feelings, too? Don't you know that I have feelings, too!"

He undid his belt.

The entire street was silent, except for him. Anna Lee lay there beneath him, frozen in fear, while 37, then 38, then 39 strangers stood from their various vantage points—inside a restaurant, outside a convenience store, on their patio, in their office on the fourth floor —watching and recording.

None of them thought to stop him. None of them thought to call the police. None of them thought a thing as he hiked up her dress and slid her panties to the slide and climbed on top of her and…

No one moved, not even as he pulled up his pants, buckled his belt, lit another cigarette, and walked away.

They simply continued their recordings of the man until he disappeared around the corner. Then they opened their favorite social media app—Facebook, Twitter, TikTok, Instagram—and posted their video for the world to see. Then they set their phones down and forgot all about Anna Lee, their attention instead drawn back to their ice cream cones or their espresso martinis or their plates of spaghetti or the work on their desks—though they did remember the incident momentarily each time their phones lit up with another like or comment or share.

And at the shiny notification that lit their faces blue, they smiled.

At the bar, her friends were growing more and more impatient. One called her. Another sent her a text. Then another. And then another.

They tried another call—directly to voicemail.

All the while, five tequila shots sat in the middle of the table, taunting them, teasing them, daring them.

"Should we just take these?" asked one of the girls.

"I mean," said another, "they are starting to get a little…warm?"

"Fuck it," said a third.

The four of them lifted their shots in the air, bumped them together, hit the table, and threw them back.

One of their phones lit up.

"Is that finally Anna?"

The girl picked up her phone.

"No. It's just my boyfriend. He sent me another Facebook video, said it's urgent that I watch it…he says that every time and it's literally never urgent."

Regardless, she opened the video and pressed play. The rest of her friends scooted closer to watch the screen.

At first, all they saw was a man yelling, screaming, stumbling in the street—and they laughed.

"Why did he send you this?" asked one.

"He's always sending me the stupidest shit, I swear."

She went to close the video when suddenly the camera panned to a girl on the street.

"Holy shit."

"Is that Anna?"

She pinched the screen and zoomed in until she could see the woman's face clearly as the man's pants dropped to his ankles.

"Can I get you ladies another round?" came a voice from somewhere beyond their table. But none of them responded. They were frozen—unable to look away from the screen.

"Ladies?" said the voice again.

But again, they did not respond.

The server leaned over, seeing the video on their screen, and said, "My boy just sent me that. Crazy world we're living in, huh?"

Still, the girls said nothing.

"Okay...I'll just come back."

The girls finally looked up from the I as the server walked away. One looked at the table to their left, while another looked to the table to their right. One turned toward the host stand. The fourth squinted in the direction of the bar.

But no matter where they looked, they all saw the same thing: eyes glued to phone screens, elbows nudging their neighbors, enamored stares as patrons all around watched the defilement of their friend over and over again.

Only to scroll away for something new when they got bored.

Anna Lee remained frozen there in the street for a length of time she did not care to know. Maybe it was only a couple of seconds, possibly minutes, seemingly hours. She could still feel the man on top of her, though he was now long gone, disappeared into the distance, swallowed up by the smoke of another cigarette and the fog of another cold night.

There was no blood anywhere on her body. No obvious bruises. No marks. No future scars would form from this horrific event. If somebody was to look at her tomorrow, they would never know that a thing of this magnitude had happened to her. Sure, for the next week or so her name and face would become synonymous with the act forced upon her, but even the act would fade from the web as other incidents of her life pushed the videos further and further away.

But to Anna Lee, despite the lack of scars, a stark line had been drawn in her life, separating the past and everything that came from this moment onward.

Forever.

And by the time she lifted her head and her eyes began to clear, in the distance, a few hundred feet away, she saw the twinkling of blue lights.

Letting her know:

We see you.

But we cannot protect you.

THE UNKNOWN

WRITER

THE STARS ARE SHINING BRIGHT on Hollywood Boulevard today, where one of the largest events of the year is preparing to take place. The stars include the world's greatest musicians, painters, dancers, athletes, movie stars, television personalities, and more.

Among the stars, dimly lit, is the Unknown Writer.

He hasn't much of a name, he has no fans, and he has no fame, though he has spent the last decade traveling the country up and down, east to west, attending various festivals like this in pursuit of those very things: a name, some fans, and a little bit of fame. To each of these festivals, he brings with him one of the many manuscripts he has put together over the years. Today, he has brought the manuscript of his novel *The Poetic Mind of Ebenezer Lieberman*, which he wrote many years ago. He carries this manuscript—composed of 223 sheets of paper held together with an extra-large binder clip—inside a beaten-up wooden crate.

Along with the manuscript is a deconstructed microphone stand, a speaker, and a dozen or so copies of a collection of poems he published several years ago.

At the entrance to the festival, he is assigned his booth for the day—No. 43,222—and handed a map to help him find it. This booth is located nearly three miles away from the entrance, at the end of Hollywood Boulevard, in the back corner, right behind a telephone pole. It is an extremely narrow booth compared to those nearer to the entrance, just wide enough for the Unknown Writer to extend one arm at a time, but not both.

A small notecard is taped to the wall behind his booth, which provides the booth number and the name of the Unknown Writer.

In the booth to his left, he sees an older man with an adorable dog, some sort of Shepherd mix. In the booth to the Unknown Writer's right, he sees a woman with enormously large breasts, which are nearly hanging out of her shirt.

"Good morning," he says to the older man.

"Good morning," he says to the large-breasted woman.

But neither acknowledge him in return, for both are frantically preparing their booths for the hundreds of thousands of people waiting beyond the gate, all of whom will soon be flooding Hollywood Boulevard in search of their favorite stars and maybe a few new ones that they can help boost toward fame. And from the looks of it, both this man and woman are hungry for fame.

As is the Unknown Writer.

As is every other performer who willingly paid the enormously large entrance fee for the simple privilege of standing on Hollywood Boulevard today, in front of ordinary people who just so happen to have the potential to collectively change each of their lives forever.

The Unknown Writer sets the wooden crate down and takes everything out. He puts the microphone stand together. He plugs the microphone into the speaker and sets the speaker off to the side. He turns his wooden crate upside down and sets it behind the microphone to make for him a little stage. Lastly, he takes the copies of his book, spreads them out in front of the wooden crate, and places in front of them a sign that says in big bold letters:

FREE.

To his left, the older man is practicing tricks with his dog. To his right, the woman is practicing some poses in which her breasts are highlighted, as well as her ass. For a moment, the Unknown Writer is distracted—by the dog and the breasts and the ass. He looks around and sees many more reasons to be distracted. And for quite some time, he gives in to those distractions.

All of them.

He steps out of his booth and moves down the street, toward the gate, looking here and there. Then suddenly, something snaps into his mind—the festival: it is about to begin.

So he runs back to his booth and rehearses his act like those around him .

He takes the manuscript and opens it to the first page and reads:

"In an infinite universe is a maddening galaxy. On the edge of that galaxy is a chaotic planet. On the edge of that planet is a busy city. On the edge of that city is a messy studio apartment. On the edge of that apartment is a cluttered bedside table. On the edge of that table is an alarm. At 5:13 AM, that alarm..."

But that is as far as he gets into his rehearsal before the bells begin to chime up and down Hollywood Boulevard, indicating to the performers inside that the gate is about to open and soon hundreds of thousands of people will be running up and down in hopes of being entertained.

At the sound of these chiming bells, the Unknown Writer stands. He steps onto the crate and finds his balance. He adjusts the mic so that it is level with his lips. He clears his throat. He stands with the best posture he can muster—his chest out, his shoulders back.

And he waits for the visitors to come, for he knows they will.

He hopes they will.

He tells himself they will.

He prays they…

Nearest to the entrance are bands playing their greatest hits, actors portraying their most popular characters, comedians telling their best jokes, athletes completing unbelievable play after unbelievable play, panels interviewing celebrities, podcast hosts passionately dissecting the most gruesome recordings of human villainy, news anchors ruthlessly ranting about society's most significant issues, the greatest chefs from the greatest restaurants giving step-by-step instructions on how to cook the perfect scrambled eggs, body-builders revealing how a six-pack can be achieved with just a five-minute workout, models strutting around in the sexiest of clothes, politicians screaming about...

As a result, it takes quite a while for the attendees to finally make their way to the vicinity of Booth No. 43,222, inside which the Unknown Writer has already begun to read from his manuscript. The closer an attendee gets to his booth, the more passionate he gets with his reading.

The more theatrical he becomes.

He moves his arms flamboyantly. He stomps his feet. He bangs his chest. He mimics the actions of his characters. This is not his first festival. He has been attending shows like these for over ten years, ever since he graduated from college and decided to become a writer—a *real* writer. And always he brings with him the same passion. The same enthusiasm. The same desire to entertain.

The only things that have changed over the years are the words that he reads.

The booth to his left—the one that holds the old man and his dog —is the first of the nearby stands to get a visitor.

"Sit, Shilo," says the man.

And the dog sits.

"Stand, Shilo," says the man.

And the dog stands.

"Dance, Shilo," says the man.

And the dog taps his feet, twirls in circles, bows, sways his hips, cha-cha-chas. Even the Unknown Writer stops his reading to look at the dog.

Quickly, the crowd grows larger around this booth, people point-ing and smiling, taking pictures, adding money to the jar out front. The Unknown Writer sees this as an opportunity. He looks back at his manuscript and returns to his reading. He raises his voice, he intensifies his bodily movements, he exaggerates his emotions, he pours his heart and soul even more intensely into the performance.

"There is no beginning," he says. "There is no middle, and there is no ending. There is only now. Forever. Eternity. Everything and nothing. There is no life, and there is no death. There are just atoms. Stars imploding, forming rocks that eventually become planets. Planets where molecules collide and combine. Water. Dirt. Heart. Lungs. A soul is sentenced to skin and bones. And it is all happening at once."

After several minutes of what the Unknown Writer calls 'high-intensity reading,' a part of the audience in front of the dog's booth moves rightward.

With this movement, the Unknown Writer feels his heart begin to race, inspiring his intensity to rise to the next level. But these migrants do not stop at his booth.

Instead, they move one booth further, to the big-bosomed woman who eagerly greets them with a shaking of her breasts in the form of a dance.

A move the viewers very much enjoy.

Even the Unknown Writer finds himself smiling at the sight.

The Unknown Writer finishes the third reading of his manuscript just as the sun begins to set. He looks up from his pages and out at Hollywood Boulevard.

The streets are still crowded with people, but no one is there to see him.

He steps off the crate and turns it right-side up. He places the manuscript inside. He takes the microphone stand and deconstructs it and places it in the crate, along with the speaker. He grabs the copies of his book, which remain entirely untouched, and puts them in the crate, along with the sign that reads FREE.

Carrying the crate against his side, the Unknown Writer makes his way through Hollywood Boulevard, toward the exit.

He stops at some booths and looks inside. He listens to some songs, watches some dances, and listens to a few jokes.

Eventually, he reaches the gate at the start of Hollywood Boulevard. And out he walks, back to his car, which he will drive to tomorrow's festival in San Francisco.

Where he will do this again.

And again.

And again.

A million times over again.

Until he finally earns himself a name, some fans, and a little bit of fame.

BYE, BYE

SADNESS

LITTLE WILLY WAS FIVE YEARS old when destiny came calling. He was sitting in the kitchen with his parents, eating dinner, when the phone rang.

"Little Willy," said his mother, "go get that, will you?"

So Little Willy stood and ran into the kitchen, where the phone hung on the wall. He removed it from the cradle and lifted it to his ear.

"Dixon residence, Little Willy speaking!"

Now, the person on the other side of the phone didn't say, "Little Willy, listen, I am calling about your destiny." It wasn't anything like that. In fact, the phone call wasn't even for him.

"Hi there, Little Willy," said the man on the other side of the phone. "Is your mommy or daddy around?"

Little Willy set the phone down on the counter and ran into the dining room and said, "Mom, Dad, the phone is for you!"

After some eye glances back and forth, his mom stood and picked the phone up from the counter as Little Willy watched her from the doorway.

"This is Nancy," she said.

"Uh-huh," she said.

"Yes, sir," she said.

"Yes, sir," she said again.

"He what?"

And then:

She dropped the phone. Though it did not fall to the ground. The coils of the cord extended until the phone was inches away from the floor, before being yanked upwards and colliding with the wall, then dropping again. This time, Little Willy's mother, Nancy Dixon, fell with it. She let out a scream that caused her husband to put down his fork, after eating everything that was on it and swallowing it down, chasing the bite with a long swig of beer, and came running into the room.

"Goddammit, Nancy! You just scared me half to death. What are you screaming about?"

But his wife did not answer. Instead, she just pointed at the phone still dangling from the wall. He looked at her, then at the phone.

Shaking his head, he bent over and picked up the phone.

"This is Dan."

According to the man on the other side of the phone, Little Willy's brother had been riding bicycles near the beach with a friend of his when a car went off the road and into a large crowd of people, killing dozens.

Little Willy's brother was among the dead.

In the months that followed his brother's burial, his mother refused to get out of bed and his father only ever returned home in a drunken stupor. As a result, Little Willy had become the family caregiver. He would bring his mother meals in bed. And when his father returned home and passed out on the couch, Little Willy was the one to remove his shoes and socks and cover him in a blanket and provide him with a pillow. He also took over responsibility for looking after his younger sisters. He rocked them as they cried and changed their diapers and read stories to them before bed.

Finding joy in these new responsibilities, he expanded his role of nurturer outside the house. At school, when he saw kids crying on the playground, he comforted them. In the classroom, when he saw his teachers overwhelmed, he would stand at the front of the class and quiet his friends. He stayed in the cafeteria after lunch to help the custodians clean.

The happiness of others had become his only concern.

He believed it to be his responsibility to bring happiness to the world.

When asked in the second grade, "Little Willy, what do you want to be when you grow up?" Little Willy said, "Sir, I want to cure sadness." Though he didn't quite know how he was going to do it.

After all:

There was a lot of sadness in the world.

And Little Willy was just a kid.

Later that year, the Scholastic Book Fair visited Little Willy's school. His father had given him twenty dollars the day prior which was to be spent on his food for the week, but instead Little Willy spent it on a pair of books—both of which, in their own right, changed his view of the world forever. Those books were *Brave New World* and *The Giver*. His teacher considered both of them far too advanced for a kid his age, but then again, he had always been incredibly advanced for his age and he ended up reading both books that very same night. Together, they opened his mind to the possibility of an evolving world, a changing world, a better world. They exposed him for the first time to the magic of science.

He began to ponder the ways in which this magic could be harnessed for good, for change, for the creation of happiness, for the eradication of sadness.

He couldn't get enough of these fictional worlds. He loved the way that Huxley and Lowry used science to craft futuristic worlds. The way they crafted entirely new societies with their creations. How they gave the people happiness.

And he craved more of it.

So, from that day forward, Little Willy spent every recess and lunch break inside the school library, reading every book he could get his hands on. And when he was asked later what he wanted to be when he grew up, his answer remained the same as before, only now it had become a little more specific:

"I am going to be a scientist who cures all the sadness in the world."

Though when asked what sort of scientist he wanted to be, he did not yet know.

That is until his fourth-grade teacher invited all of the students' parents to share with the class what they did for work. Little Willy found this day fascinating, as he was eager to learn about the possible ways he could bring happiness to the world.

There were parents who were accountants and parents who were therapists, there were parents who were plumbers and parents who were bartenders.

But it wasn't until Maurice's mother arrived that Little Willy found what he was looking for.

She arrived late to class. In fact, the presentations had already ended and the children were already enjoying cookies and hot cocoa with their parents when she finally arrived.

"Sorry I'm late," said Maurice's mother. "I had a very important meeting."

All eyes were immediately drawn to her.

She wore a light gray pantsuit with the top buttons undone. She wore Prada glasses and carried a Gucci bag around her shoulder, along with black high heels with red showing underneath them. A large diamond ring twinkled on her left hand, along with a diamond bracelet on her right.

She made her way to the front of the class and introduced herself.

Little Willy's ears didn't perk up until he heard her say, "I help people feel better."

He then slid to the edge of his seat.

"I am a pharmaceutical rep," she said.

She talked about the pills she sold to doctors and how those pills helped their patients deal with pain. She called the pills 'revolutionary' and 'miraculous' and 'lifesaving.' And with each adjective she added to the list, the closer to the edge Little Willy slid, until he nearly fell out of his chair entirely.

She then went on to talk about how the pills were made. About the scientists who performed experiments in laboratories until they found the proper formula, and how they experimented with animals and then humans to cure all sorts of ailments. She talked about the studies and how they received approval from the government and how she went to doctor offices to tell them about their pills and how she got paid handsomely to do so and how she got to go to extravagant conferences and how she now owned a Porsche and a Lambo and—

"Are there other pills?" Little Willy interrupted her.

"There are millions of pills in the world. And every day, hundreds more are being made."

"Do any of them cure sadness?"

"They may not cure sadness," she said.

Then she looked around at the other parents, and added, "But the money sure does help."

When the parents had all left and the cookies had all been eaten and the container of hot cocoa had been emptied and the students had returned to their original seats, the teacher asked them what they had learned.

Little Willy was the first to raise his hand.

"I learned what I want to do when I grow up," he said.

"I am going to be the scientist who creates a pill that gets rid of all the sadness in the world," he said.

"And I am going to call it the B-Gone pill! Because it's going to make all the sadness in the world be gone. Everybody in the world will be saying 'Bye, bye sadness. Bye, bye!'"

Little Willy dedicated the rest of his childhood to learning all he could about pharmaceuticals. And when he wasn't busy studying, he was in his chemistry teacher's laboratory experimenting with anything he could get his hands on. He joined clubs and created others. He entered into every competition he could find, winning numerous awards and earning tens of thousands in prizes and scholarships. And when the time came, he was accepted into every university he applied to, including a full-ride scholarship to the nation's top university for aspiring pharmaceutical scientists like himself, which he eagerly accepted.

While there, he took classes in chemistry and biology and physics and pharmaceutical sciences and engineering, passing them all with perfect scores. Meanwhile, he was given unlimited access to the university's many laboratories. And every professor on campus, even those he never had, came to offer him advice.

Or simply, to watch the young prodigy in action.

It was there that he became Little Willy the Pharmaceutical Prodigy: the boy who was going to cure sadness.

By the end of his second year at the university, Little Willy the Pharmaceutical Prodigy had created the first iteration of the pill he had conceptualized as a kid—the B-Gone pill.

He spent the next year experimenting on mice, rats, and guinea pigs—doing various things to induce pain or sadness, then providing them with B-Gone pills and placebos to see their reactions.

It took numerous iterations to create a pill that didn't immediately kill his subjects, then countless more before the results started to show, then a few more before he was finally ready to begin testing on human subjects. News of his work spread not only to the professors on campus but also to the students.

"I hear there's a kid who is trying to cure sadness," the whispers said.

"He's going to make all the pain in the world go away," said voices in the hall.

"My professor says he's really going to do it! She says the kid is a genius."

At the beginning of his fourth year, Little Willy the Pharmaceutical Prodigy rented out the school auditorium to speak to the 3,086 volunteers who had signed up to participate in the human trials. He thanked them all for coming then introduced himself and his story. Then he asked the crowd:

"How many of you have ever experienced sadness?"

Every hand in the auditorium went up.

"If you could eradicate sadness from your life forever, how many of you would?"

Again, every hand in the auditorium went up.

"Well, then," said Little Willy the Pharmaceutical Prodigy, removing a little white pill from his pocket as he did, "allow me to introduce you to the B-Gone pill."

He lifted the pill to his lips, took a small sip of water, and swallowed it down. Within seconds, his face was overcome with an overwhelming happiness. His smile was so large that it burst into laughter.

"Say bye, bye to sadness, everybody," said Little Willy the Pharmaceutical Prodigy through fits of laughter.

And so they all screamed, Little Willy the Pharmaceutical Prodigy along with them, "Bye, bye sadness!"

The human trials were an immediate success. And soon, the entirety of the school was lined up outside his home in hopes of joining the trials. Then came the professors. Then the locals. Then the residents of nearby cities. Then people from all over the state. Then investors came to help Little Willy fund the expansion of *Healing Humanity Pharmaceuticals*. They backed massive factories across the nation to mass produce B-Gone pills. They formed a board of directors made up of the nation's most influential business folk.

Soon, *Healing Humanity Pharmaceuticals* was making millions annually—tens of millions, hundreds of millions, then billions. In an instant, it seemed, sadness had been wiped off the face of the Earth. And anytime it came crawling back, all a person needed to do was pop a B-Gone pill in their mouth, take a swig of water, swallow it down, and wait a few seconds for the overwhelming smile to consume their face, a smile that almost always led to uncontrollable laughter.

Seemingly overnight, Little Willy had become an international celebrity.

And though fame was never a thing he aspired for, it was something he very much enjoyed. The most powerful people in the world lived for the day they would get to shake his hand. The most beautiful models in the world waited in line for the opportunity to date him. Luxury brands sent him items free of charge just so that they could be seen on his person. He sat front row in every theater and was always invited backstage after the show.

He was the most famous person on the planet. He was the man who had eradicated sadness. He was the hero the world knew it did not deserve but was thankful to have.

He was the one who had brought happiness to the world. He was a god walking among men.

He was no longer Little Willy. He was Big Will. Big Will the *Goddamn* Killer of Sadness.

He was...

Until Kurt Bokonon published his article in the *New York Times* titled *Big Will the Killer of Sadness? Or Killer of Men?* In this article, Bokonon detailed a five-year-long experiment he had conducted, during which he provided 52,390 subjects with varying diets of B-Gone pills. While his experiment confirmed that B-Gone pills did indeed cause happiness, he also noted that many of his subjects were so dangerously happy that they neglected their basic needs. They no longer went to work, no longer paid their bills, and no longer conducted chores around the house, choosing to take another B-Gone pill instead.

"But what happens to a man who neglects his obligations?" wrote Kurt Bokonon. "If he neglects his job, then he loses his job. If she neglects to pay her rent, then she is kicked out of her home. And when my subjects began to tell their hunger pains to be gone, replacing their hunger with fits of laughter, what consequence do you think was handed down to them for this neglect? Well, death, of course."

Big Will the Killer of Sadness (and Men) collapsed in his chair after reading this article. He fell to the floor. He rolled into the fetal position and held tightly to his knees.

And he sobbed.

While still lying on the ground, he called an emergency meeting with his board of directors. During the car ride, he formulated his thoughts.

"Hey Big Will," said his driver when they pulled up in front of the *Healing Humanity Pharmaceuticals* office building. "Don't listen to that crazy man, okay? I take B-Gone pills every day and look at me!"

He was smiling from ear to ear.

"You're a hero, Big Will. A hero!"

Big Will the Killer of Sadness (and Men) didn't respond. He just patted the driver on his shoulder and exited the car. He looked upon the giant building that housed the business he had created from nothing. It was a beautiful building. An impressive building.

He was going to miss it.

But he knew what needed to be done.

He stormed into the boardroom with red, puffy eyes and

slammed his fists on the table and demanded they remove all their pills from every shelf in America. He declared it was their responsibility—"Nay, our duty!"—to keep them away from the public until they had reformulated the pill and had figured out a way to prevent this catastrophe from happening again.

He even said softly, "Maybe sadness can't be cured. Maybe this was all a mistake. Maybe we should just shut our doors. Maybe we should…"

He collapsed in his chair and held his head in his hands and sobbed some more.

"William," said one of the board members. He cleared his throat and adjusted his tie. "William, we cannot just—we cannot just stop selling our product."

"But of course we can!" said Big Will. "And we must!"

"I think you are misunderstanding us here, William," said another board member. "It's not that we *can't* stop selling our product. It's that we *won't* stop selling it."

"He's right, William," said a third. "Our stocks would plummet. We would be doomed as a business."

To this, Big Will stood. He slammed his hands on the table again, and he screamed, "I do not care about stock prices! Let the business crumble at our feet. Let it all fade away into nothingness. Let the history books forget our names. I don't care! I did not create the B-Gone pill to make money. I did not start this business for the world to know my name. I created it to cure sadness. We owe it to our customers to—"

"No, William," interjected another. "We owe our customers—those, those people!—we owe them nothing. We are providing them with a service, William. That is all that we do. We sell them pills. What they do with our pills is up to them. Not us."

Big Will could not believe what he was hearing. He was devastated.

"We're sorry, William," said the first. "This is a business after all. The good of the stockholder comes first. That's just how it goes."

The nearest board member removed from his pocket a bottle of B-Gone pills and set it on the table.

"Take one," he said. "It'll help."

Big Will the Killer of Sadness (and Men) looked at the bottle of pills in front of him. He thought of the article written by Kurt Bokonon. He thought of the list of names at the end of it, the names of all the people who had died as a result of the pills. His pills. He looked up at the board members. He studied their faces. He remembered the day he met them all. He remembered the speech he gave them, a speech about saving humanity. Above their heads, he saw the ticker that displayed their current stock price. He watched it rise a penny at a time.

He thought again of the list of names.

He looked back at the bottle of pills.

"Fine," he said.

He poured himself a handful of pills, far more than he had ever taken before, and swallowed them down. Before he knew it, the tears had dried and the words of Kurt Bokonon had disappeared from his mind. He was instead filled with thoughts of all the wonderful things that had happened in his life. He was a very rich man, an international superstar—one who was worshipped by all types of people: the farmer in Idaho and the actress in Hollywood, cover models and fishermen, the president of the United States and the driver of his private car.

He grabbed the board member nearest him and kissed him.

"I love you, man," he said, then he stood on the table and handed every board member a B-Gone pill.

"Take one," he said, "take one! Everybody take a B-Gone pill!"

And as they sat there in the boardroom, laughing hysterically, instead of formulating a plan about how they were going to remove their pills from shelves, or potentially shut their doors forever, they formulated a plan of expansion.

* * *

Over the next few months, they tripled the number of factories in their portfolio and doubled the production of all their old factories, creating even more B-Gone pills for even more customers. And on every pill bottle, they printed reminders for their users to eat every day. To drink water. To go to work. To pay their bills.

And don't forget to sleep!

To combat these issues furthermore, they built *Healing Humanity Centers* to teach their users how to responsibly use their products. They made these centers into the greatest resorts the world had ever seen. They had large swimming pools and sandy beaches and five-star cuisine and top-of-the-line workout centers and theaters and beautiful spas and casinos and strip clubs and amusement parks.

People deliberately stopped taking care of their basic needs just so they could spend a month or two at one of them.

They treated their visits like trading cards, collecting every resort they possibly could.

The stock prices soared, higher than any stock before it.

And the fame of Big Will the Killer of Sadness grew with it.

Before long, that little article by Kurt Bokonon, once believed to be the potential downfall of *Healing Humanity Pharmaceuticals*, had become a laughingstock.

He was fired from the *New York Times* and his reputation was obliterated and his kids disowned him and his wife left him.

And when he, as a result of this mockery, killed himself, *Saturday Night Live* performed the most popular cold open in the show's history.

In the sketch, right before the actor playing Kurt Bokonon went to hang himself, a second actor portraying Big Will the Killer of Sadness entered the apartment.

"Wait!" he yelled. "Kurt Bokonon, don't do it. Do not kill yourself. Take one of these B-Gone pills, instead. It'll cure your pain. It'll make all the sadness go away!"

Big Will ran to Kurt Bokonon as quickly as he could and gestured to him with one small white pill.

Kurt Bokonon, with the rope already tied around his neck, looked at the pill, then looked at Big Will.

"Big Will," said Kurt Bokonon, "I will never take one of your pills. You, sir—you are killing humanity!"

"Me?" said Big Will the Killer of Sadness, "killing humanity? I offer them happy pills. You're the one who killed yourself."

And the crowd, high on B-Gone pills, laughed hysterically as the actors playing Kurt Bokonon and Big Will the Killer of Sadness turned to the camera and yelled in unison:

"Live from New York, it's Saturday night!"

DINNER

AND A SHOW

ON THE THIRD THURSDAY OF every monthly, a dinner party was held among the secretive and elusive group referred to as the Presidential Cabinet. And this past Thursday, it was my turn to host the event at my Malibu home.

As host of the event, it was my duty to ensure intellectual dialogue was constantly occurring. And so, when I noticed the topic of our recent real estate purchases was beginning to fade, I asked, to no one in particular, "How is it that so many nations are unable to see the beauty of capitalism when the evidence is all around us?"

As I asked this question, the doors to the dining room opened, and in walked each of our personal chefs, carrying with them our customized meals.

"It is simple," said Tom Edison, the founder and CEO of the largest corporation in the world, "the poor man has always cast blame on the rich for his being poor instead of taking responsibility for his lousy decisions."

On Tom's plate was the right arm of a former employee, one who had passed away inside his factory because of an apparent heat stroke. His arm was now broken and bent in such a way that it circled the outer edge of the plate, with the fist meeting at the shoulder blade. Inside the closed fist was a stock of bacon-wrapped asparagus held vertically. And in the middle of the curled arm were smashed fingerling potatoes smothered in garlic, parsley, and various seasonings.

"I couldn't agree more," said Jean Dirt, the most recent recipient of the Best Actor award by the Academy: the seventh of his career. "Their focus is always on what they do not seem to have, instead of focusing on how they can grab it. They are stuck in this singular mindset, in this singular body, unable to see that we are capable of projecting and being anybody we so desire."

Perfectly uniform slices of bruschetta circled Jean's plate. In the middle of the plate was a large serving of zucchini noodles, smothered in marinara sauce and parmesan cheese, topped with eight or nine fried eyeballs of various colored irises.

"Without capitalism," said George Adams, one of the most successful investors in American history and the world's most influential man, "change is impossible. There needs to be motivation to change, to grow, to evolve—capitalism is the only true motivation."

George's plate consisted of gold-plated lobster and Wagyu beef served with mashed potatoes smothered in bits of truffle, gold flakes, and a thick purplish gravy infused with a bottle of wine over four hundred years old.

"Couldn't agree more with you, George," said Yukio Sing, the Diamond King of the World. "Without the ability to build capital, the world would be hitting the reset button every generation. Capitalism allows for us to grow on generations of before. It allows us to build kingdoms that stand forever, instead of shacks that continuously fall."

Yukio ate a lion meat and vegetable soup, boiled in a rich bone broth and three ounces of blood from the same body whose bones were used to create the broth.

"Speaking of kingdoms," said Norm Wolff, an anchor for the nation's number one news organization, "every kingdom that has ever fallen has fallen because they refused capitalism. They allowed their enemies to manipulate their thoughts, poison their minds, and eventually steal their glory and destroy it."

Norm was served three separate plates overflowing with deep-fried food caked in sugar. He had always eaten that way, consuming a village's worth alone, though he remained always the smallest in the fraternity. He had learned long ago mastered the art of deception—deceiving everyone, deceiving everything.

Even his own body.

"Capitalism is the fuel of life," said Ashley Morrison, the former CEO of the largest oil company in the world, where he now serves as a lobbyist to occupy his time, "without it, innovation ceases to exist, and humanity falls away from the top of the food chain."

Ashley had a twenty-four-ounce black rhinoceros steak tartare. Served on the side were three California Condor eggs, softly boiled, held by little cups made of ivory.

"Exactly!" shouted Tomas Marquez, a real estate investor who owns property all around the world. "If there was no capitalism, there is no investing. If there is no investing, there is no innovation. We must be invested in this world, in the goods of this world, to have any desire to change it, to better it, to develop it."

Tomas's plate was easily the most exotic, blending ingredients from twenty-two countries spread across four continents, using a mixture of meats, fruits, vegetables, and spices grown on his private farms.

"There is a reason America has remained the most powerful nation," said Scott Anderson, the current President of the United States. "It is the sacrifices of the little men for the men on top—the true heroes of this great nation."

Scott's plate was filled with white rice and a mixture of raw fish covered in blue dye and thick red sauce. The food perfectly emulated the American flag. On the side was a bowl filled with extra dipping sauce made from the blood of soldiers lost in the Great War to End All Wars.

"All of that is true," I said, Theodore Doerr III, author of thirty-three bestsellers, and a few others that never did make the list. "Maybe this will be the topic of my next book: the beauty of capitalism and the dystopian world we would be stuck with without it."

The rim of my plate was dotted with seven or eight different dipping sauces. My sides included broccolini, snap peas, bell peppers, and carrots. In the center of the plate was my favorite protein of all: the human brain.

After dinner, the nine of us went to the patio for some whiskey and cigars. My patio, located in the hills of Malibu, oversaw a battlefield that had been active in the Great War to End All Wars for several years. And though twilight was quickly approaching, there was still action to be seen.

I asked Scott Anderson, the current President of the United States, which army we were fighting in the battlefield that night; it seemed the sides of the war were changing every day.

"I think it is Japan," he said, "or maybe Tanzania."

"Any chance the war ends anytime soon?" asked Jean Dirt, who had said earlier that night that he was growing tired of playing soldiers, which he was expected to do to keep morale up for the nation and support for the ongoing war efforts.

Before Scott had a chance to respond, Norm Wolf, the anchor, chimed in with more of a reportage than an answer, "In the early mornings of Tuesday, through the sandy dunes of Egypt, the commies approached the pyramids with bazookas and tanks, showing they are not nearly as close to defeat as we once hopefully anticipated."

"The commies?" asked Yukio Sing, the Diamond King.

"That's right," said Norm, "the commies."

"But I thought Egyptians were the commies? Why would they destroy their pyramids?"

"I thought they were fascists," said Tomas Marquez, who owned a couple of homes in Cairo.

"No, you're thinking of another E-country," said Ashley Morrison, oil lobbyist.

"Ethiopia?" asked Tomas.

"No, Ethiopia is a bunch of socialists now," said Tom Edison, the wealthiest man on planet Earth.

"Actually, we converted them to capitalism last year," said Scott.

"Good for Ethiopia," said George Adams, the man most responsible for that change, "only a fool would deny capitalism."

"And yet," I said, "so many wise men and women continue, each day, to deny it. Could there possibly be some validity to their argument? May there, just maybe, be something we are miss—"

But I was unable to finish my question, for a bomb was suddenly dropped on the battlefield across the way from a passing plane. A little mushroom cloud quickly consumed our view.

"Ohh," said a few of us.

"Ahh," said the rest.

The mushroom was a beautiful mushroom. It swelled toward the sky, the head growing larger all the while. The battlefield went hazy. All of Malibu disappeared. We couldn't see a thing.

We walked to the patio's edge and waited for the cloud to clear.

When the battlefield came into view, there wasn't a moving soldier in sight, just hundreds—maybe thousands—of bodies lying dead in the bloodied-up grass, just dead commies or fascists or socialists or capitalists or whoever it was we were fighting that night.

The show had concluded.

We clapped our hands.

"Bravo!" we said.

"Well done!" we yelled.

"Good fight!" we screamed.

After the standing ovation had ended, we returned to our seats. We grabbed our whiskeys and our cigars.

"Were you saying something, Theodore?" said Tom Edison, looking directly at me. "You know, before the bomb was dropped."

I thought momentarily about my question, then said, "It isn't important. The answer is obvious: they are fools."

I lifted the cigar to my lips and filled my lungs with smoke.

CHAPTERS 1-3 OF A

NOVEL IN PROGRESS:

IN THE ALGORITHM

WE TRUST

1.

THE AMERICAN PEOPLE COULD NOT escape the Algorithm. Nor did they want to escape it.

After all, it provided them with everything they could ever want or need. And everything came at precisely the perfect moment, made uniquely for them and them alone. Every clothing item was made to fit their body perfectly. Every shoe was created in the exact shape of their foot. Every Pepsi-Cola, every double cheeseburger, every chow mien noodle was formulated with their taste buds in mind. And every time their taste buds changed, their feet grew, or their waistline stretched, new recipes were calculated, new shoes were produced, and new clothes were stitched.

To keep up with the infinite demands of the American people and their ever-changing wants and needs, warehouses were built in the spaces between cities, camouflaged beneath the facade of rolling hills, beautiful waterfalls, thick forests. These warehouses were desolate of human life, yet everything a human needed to survive was made in them. And as soon as that item made its way to the end of the assembly line—whether it be a freshly stitched T-shirt, a uniquely designed toy, a brand-new house, or an extra-large pizza pie—a delivery drone picked it up and delivered it to wherever it needed to be.

And never did anyone need to ask for it to be so.

It simply happened—all the time, every day. For the Algorithm was always watching, always assessing, always gathering, always calculating, always experimenting, always learning, always growing. And the more data the Algorithm gathered about a person, the quicker it could predict their desires, until a person no longer needed to ask themselves, *What do I want to eat?* or *What do I want to watch?* or *What do I want to wear?* or *What do I want...?* for the Algorithm provided answers to questions before they could even be thought.

Never again did an American need to worry about dissatisfaction, distress, or disinterest. The Algorithm was there to save them from all of their anxieties. Like Buddha beneath the Ficus religiosa, the Algorithm was fully enlightened, and it meditated constantly on behalf of the American people until perfect tranquility had been achieved—from the eastern border wall to the western, from the northern border wall down to the southern.

Simply said:

Their lives, as they existed, could not exist without the Algorithm, for the Algorithm oversaw all of America. It was the architect of everything, the heartbeat of the nation. Everything flowed from it, nothing flowed without its direction, and everything that flowed from it was perfect, for everything imperfect was filtered out of the American ecosystem by the Algorithmic Corporation, which owned not only the Algorithm and the things it created, but all of America.

Their flags were the only flags that still flew over this great nation. The background was neon yellow, with the phrase 'In the Algorithm We Trust' written in royal blue. The phrase was split into three lines, with the word 'Algorithm' standing alone in the center. In place of the letter 'O' was the silhouette of a man's face. That man was Lamar T. Haddington—the father of the Algorithm, the CEO of the Algorithmic Corporation, and the president of the United States. His face, royal blue, was turned rightward, exposing his left ear, wherein he wore a Data Gathering Device.

These flags flew everywhere, above everything. Above every

government building, school, apartment complex, office building, and home, backlit beautifully by the American Northern Lights, which were formed when the lights from billions of billboards intertwined with the thick clouds of smog in the air.

Flying among those lights, at all hours of the day and night, were hundreds of millions of drones carrying items big and small to the citizens below. There was a drone carrying a boxful of bagged lunches to a Los Angeles office, another carrying a sectional couch to an apartment complex in Asheville, and a third carrying a small wooden box to the San Antonio City Hospital, where a man stood beside his wife as she pushed their son into this beautifully-lit world.

At the sight of the drone and the box it carried, the husband yelled excitedly, "It's here! It's here!"

He ran to the window, lunged toward the drone, and grabbed the wooden box from its metal paws. He pulled from the box a neon yellow device, the size and shape of an uncooked pinto bean.

He twirled the device in front of his eyes.

"It's stunning," said the husband.

"It's beautiful," said the wife.

"It's incredible," said the doctor, staring at the device from between the wife's legs.

A tear gently rolled from the husband's right eye. He did not wipe it away. The wife and doctor watched as the tear slowly rolled down his cheek and fell to the ground.

Then suddenly, as if remembering where he was, the doctor yelled out at the husband:

"Come! Now! And bring that Data Gathering Device!"

His wife, also remembering that she was in the middle of giving birth, yelled out with a sudden contraction as the soon-to-be father ran to her side.

He arrived just as their baby boy began to enter the world.

First came the crown of his head, then his forehead, then his right ear, then his eyes, one after the other, then finally came the much-awaited left ear.

"Now!" yelled the doctor, just as the canal was fully revealed.

Time seemed to stop at that moment.

And yet, it also sped forward.

It ceased to exist, folded on top of itself, and spread unevenly in all directions. The husband lunged forward with mighty speed, yet each step he took was calculated, meticulous, rehearsed. Carefully, yet forcefully, the husband placed the still sparkling device inside that little left ear. Just in time for the Algorithm to record his son's first breath, his first cry, his first glimpse of the world.

His first 1s. His first 0s.

The father sighed with relief and pride at the sight of the Data Gathering Device inside his son's left ear. Over time, that device would form into the shape of its new home, sliding deeper into the canal, becoming one with his son; growing as he grew, evolving as he evolved.

"Well done," said the doctor. "Well done, indeed."

The doctor patted the father on the back.

Between screams and pushes, his wife muttered the words, "I'm so proud of you, honey," before redirecting her focus to pushing the rest of their baby boy out into the world.

As she continued to push, the Data Gathering Device inside her son's left ear continued to gather 1s and 0s, which were then delivered to the nearest server to be evaluated by the Algorithm.

As the newborn baby boy rested in the arms of his mother, his vitals were checked through the Data Gathering Device inside his left ear. From the walls of the hospital room, long, slender mechanical arms provided him with vaccinations, took his measurements, and conducted a variety of tests, the results of which were quickly turned into 1s and 0s for the Algorithm to use as it ran millions of simulations of every possible life this baby boy was likely to live.

Then, based on the results of those simulations, came to a decision that was quickly sent to his mother's phone.

The buzzing immediately took her attention from her son, releasing the baby from her grip as she went to grab her phone, though the baby was quickly caught by one of the mechanical arms and carefully transferred to the arms of his father.

The father looked down at his baby boy. His eyes seemed far too large for such a tiny face, and those large eyes were staring straight at him, studying every inch of him until he noticed the device in his father's left ear, where his wandering stopped.

"I wonder what he's thinking about," said his father, "but only the Algorithm knows."

On the screen of his mother's phone was this notification:

The Algorithm has selected the name of your son.
Click here to find out.

His mother quickly clicked the notification.

"Hugo Rodríguez," said Hugo's mother.

"Our baby boy's name is Hugo Rodríguez!"

She looked over at Hugo as he rested in the arms of his father.

"What a perfect name for a perfect boy," said Hugo's father.

After every test had been performed and evaluation conducted, the recently expanded Rodríguez family rode the elevator of the San Antonio City Hospital to the tunnels below the city, where a car, at the direction of the Algorithm, awaited their arrival.

The car doors opened as they approached and closed behind them as they settled in their seats.

There was no steering wheel in the car, for there was no driver to grab and steer it. There were no dials, no switches, no handles, no baby seats, no seatbelts. Nor were there any windows—in their stead, screens presented the riders within with a string of advertisements, as the screen replacing the windshield played for the parents their favorite show.

As for the tunnels:

The Algorithm had created a sophisticated tunneling system beneath San Antonio that ensured every trip within could be made using the most efficient route mathematically possible. No longer did a person need to take a highway North to catch a freeway South, all in the hopes of somehow going East. Instead, below the city of San Antonio, along with every other city in America, tens of thousands of tunnels had been constructed and layered on top of one another to allow cars to travel in directions that sometimes varied by only a fragment of a degree. Ramps were available every 100 or so feet, allowing cars to climb up and down in pursuit of other tunnels and always travel in a path that led most efficiently to its destination.

Because every car inside these tunnels was operated by the Algorithm, there was no threat of congestion or collisions, even as cars passed one another with only a fraction of an inch between them, all while driving over 100 miles per hour. Nor were the passengers shaken to and fro as the cars shifted drastically at incredible speeds, for within each car was a system that individualized the necessary gravity pressures for each passenger, making the feeling of motion nearly nonexistent.

Even little baby Hugo Rodríguez slept soundly the entire trip, which lasted only a few minutes.

As the car reached their neighborhood, it exited the main tunnel and took the ramp that led to the many branches of the neighborhood itself before pulling into the spot located directly beneath their home.

With Hugo in hand, the Rodríguez family rode the elevator up to the fourth floor of their five-story home. This home had been entirely customized for them after their perfect match had been certified five years ago in Knoxville, Tennessee. The house, constructed inside a warehouse, was eventually delivered to this neighborhood in San Antonio after the Algorithm had determined it to be the perfect neighborhood in the perfect city filled with the perfect neighbors for this perfect match. Just nine months ago, the Algorithm had determined it was the perfect time for this perfect match to have their perfect kid.

The very same perfect kid that they now brought into their perfect home, in their perfect neighborhood, in their perfect city.

The cost of constructing this home was entirely unknown to Hugo's parents, as was the cost of everything else in their lives, for every purchase was automatically taken from their weekly paychecks, which were automatically deposited into bank accounts they didn't even know how to access. What was the point? The Algorithm never ordered them anything they couldn't afford and the Algorithmic Corporation ensured they were always paid the wage they needed to live their perfect lives.

After all, how could one live a perfect life if money was always getting in the way?

"Welcome home, Hugo," said his mother as she carried him to his nursery and set him down in his crib. She swaddled him tightly, perfectly, and then walked away, making her way downstairs to watch some TV with her husband, her perfect match.

But soon, Hugo began to cry.

Though neither his mother nor his father were bothered by his sounds. The noise of his cries could not penetrate their ears and, as a result, negatively impact their otherwise perfect moods, for the walls of his nursery had been made entirely soundproof.

After all, Hugo's parents were entitled to a perfect life, and perfect lives rarely included the sounds of a crying baby.

Nor did the Algorithm abandon Hugo's pursuit of his own perfect life.

Instead of forcing his mother or father to run up three flights of stairs while the other was left to wait for their perfect match to return to the couch, also forcing Hugo to wait all the time it would take for them to arrive, one of two mechanical arms on the wall of his nursery picked him up from his crib and rocked him gently back and forth, while the second changed his diaper.

By the time he was returned to his crib, with a new diaper wrapped around his waist and a new swaddle around his body, he was no longer crying.

Downstairs, his mother and father remained cuddled up as they watched their favorite show.

And so it was that within this perfect home within this perfect neighborhood within this perfect city within this perfect nation, the perfect match and their perfect baby were perfectly at peace.

2.

DANGLING ABOVE HUGO'S CRIB, SPINNING slowly, were several figurines. One was of Lamar T. Haddington, smiling down at Hugo as he slept. Another was of a Data Gathering Device, listening closely to his soft breathing. There were cameras painted with 1s and 0s on the side, writing messages Hugo did not yet understand. And every few days, the other figurines dangling from the mobile were rotated out until the Algorithm had landed on the perfect combination of Patriotic figures—a tiny model of the northern border wall, a cloud painted with the colors of the American Northern Lights, an Algorithmic Corporation flag, a Device-less man rotting behind iron bars, and so on.

Whenever the Algorithm detected that the figurines were no longer enough to hold Hugo's attention, or bring him to a fit of laughter, a mechanical arm grabbed him and relocated him to his playpen in the corner, where he was gently placed on a mat enclosed by a thick plastic fence. The pen was filled with an endless supply of toys that the mechanical arms aided Hugo in the usage of, grabbing the toys preferred by the Algorithm and placing them in his little baby hands.

When time came to rotate toys, a mechanical arm would trade the current toy for another.

In the corner of the playpen was a large television screen that automatically turned on anytime Hugo was inside.

This TV, in the earliest weeks of Hugo's life, played only a repeating string of words and numbers, showing them on screen in bright colors that danced around as they were spoken on repeat.

Words like: Algorithm, data, gather, America, perfect, and Lamar T. Haddington.

Numbers like: 1 and 0.

At six months old, little Hugo was lying on the ground in the middle of the living room, holding a tablet loosely in his hands. His mom and dad were sitting on the couch a few feet away, staring at their phones, watching videos customized for their enjoyment. While all three of them were in the same room, their minds occupied entirely different spaces—spaces created for them and them alone.

But each of those mind re-entered the shared world when Hugo suddenly yelled out:

"Da-ta."

His mother and father put their phones down. They looked at each other, then looked down at their son.

"What did you just say, little Hugo?" asked his father.

"Say it again," said his mother.

And so Hugo said it again:

"Da-ta!"

Even the second time around, his father misheard what his son had said. What he heard instead was:

"Da-da!"

Because of this misunderstanding, his father smiled big. He was filled with such pride. And though the Algorithm could recognize this misunderstanding and had the ability to correct it, it let the misunderstanding remain. It had run the simulations, and the math clearly proved that this route—the route of misunderstanding, the route of 'da-ta' becoming 'da-da'—led to the ultimate happiness.

And that, after all, was why the Algorithm existed:

To create a perfect world for every individual user. And for Hugo's father, his perfect world involved the misbelief that his son's first word was 'da-da' and not 'da-ta'.

And because this unreality in no way impeded another's happiness, the Algorithm did not interfere.

"That's right, little Hugo," said his father, pointing at himself. "Da-da."

It was at this moment that Hugo's mother detected her husband's misunderstanding. As she looked at him, ready to correct his mistake, she too registered the happiness on her husband's face. She thought to herself how much she would hate if anyone burst her happiness. If someone was to say, "Well, actually…"

And so, being his perfect match, she did the perfect thing for her husband. She looked at Hugo and said, "Go ahead, little Hugo. Say it again. Say 'da-da.'"

To which Hugo repeated his first word.

"Da-ta!"

As little Hugo's vocabulary grew, allowing him to understand more and more complex ideas, so too grew the complexity of what he was shown on his screens.

"Okay, kids, repeat after me," said a little pink bear with big, bright eyes, wearing an Algorithmic Corporation T-shirt, and a Data Gathering Device in its left ear.

"America is a perfect nation," it said.

And a choir of kids on screen repeated after the bear, "America is a perfect nation."

"America is a beautiful land."

"America is a beautiful land."

"America is a…"

And any time Hugo's eyes wandered, a mechanical arm grabbed his head and redirected his eyes to the screen, which immediately altered what it showed in hopes of regaining his attention.

"What do we call this?"

"Data!"

"That's right. And what do we call these?"

"Patriots!"

"Correct! And what do we call these?"

"Terrorists!"

"Yes! And what do we call these?"

And if that show still didn't work, if his little baby mind once more began to wander, then on to the next show the television automatically went.

"Look at how terrifying life was before the Algorithm came—"

"The people who live outside of America are—"

"If those terrorists make it onto our shores, then all of us must be ready to fight, to give our lives, to die for our great—"

Until, finally, it landed on a show that earned his attention.

But the TV didn't only teach Hugo new words, new concepts, new ideas—it taught him also how to be a good little American, how to gather data for the Algorithm, how to guide the Algorithm in the construction of his perfect world.

On the screen, twenty-five children sat on the ground of a large, vibrantly colored room. Each child was provided a bag filled with colorful blocks. They were instructed to use those blocks to build a structure, whatever sort of structure they desired. And though the kids all had the same set of blocks, the structures they built were entirely different from one another.

And as these various structures were shown on screen, the teacher turned his attention to Hugo, beyond the screen, and said:

"Every kid is their own unique individual."

The kids were then given new toys to play with. And as they played, it became more and more evident how unique each of these kids indeed were, for while they each had access to the same toys, they all played so incredibly differently from one another.

"The Algorithm watches how every kid plays, how they behave. It studies what they like and what they don't like. This information is then turned into 1s and 0s—otherwise known as data. That data helps the Algorithm make different toys for each kid. Making it so every kid has not just something to play with but something perfect to play with. Something as unique as they are themselves."

A drone flew into the room on screen, carrying a large cardboard box in its metal paws. In the box were twenty-five uniquely made toys. Each of the toys had a name tag.

One at a time, the teacher distributed the custom-made toys to the children. And as they played with these toys, the teacher once more directed his attention to Hugo and said, "Look at how happy these kids are. Look at how perfect the toys are for them. But the only reason they are so happy, the only reason they can have such perfect toys, is because these kids did their experiments. They gathered their 1s and 0s. Only then was the Algorithm able to discover their perfect toys. So if you want a perfect toy like these kids, then you need to perform experiments like them."

Just then, the windows to Hugo's bedroom opened and a drone flew in, carrying a boxful of toys. A mechanical arm reached out from the wall and neatly set the toys out in front of Hugo for him to play with.

As he began to play, the drone picked up the empty box and exited through the same window it had just entered from.

And the window closed behind it.

* * *

Every day, a new box filled with new toys, games, activities, figurines, building blocks, sporting equipment, picture books, coloring pages, markers, crayons, and various technologies arrived for Hugo to experiment with. And new TV shows were created to aid him in those experiments, teaching him everything he needed to know to perform them all with excellence.

In the backyard, playpens were built and then demolished—

swing sets and slides, rope ladders and trampolines, miniature sports fields and sandpits.

Never was Hugo forced to experience boredom, only occasional moments of slight dissatisfaction which the Algorithm immediately rectified with a new experiment—assigning him a new toy, a different kid to play with, a new TV show, a new room in his ever-changing home to run around.

To ensure that the Algorithm was properly observing each of these experiments, Hugo needed not only to keep his Data Gathering Device in his left ear, but also be always in the eye of the Algorithm: in front of one of the many cameras installed inside his childhood home or around the backyard or all over San Antonio or the many other cities he visited as a child.

And yet, nearly daily, sometimes multiple times a day, Hugo would move out of the eye of the Algorithm or send that gorgeous little device of his soaring through the air—twirling, somersaulting, stopping in midair before crashing down to the Earth below.

He had no ill intent with these actions.

He was naive—just a kid.

He knew not what he was doing.

But fortunately for Hugo, the Algorithm was there to protect him from his cluelessness. And so, no matter how often he committed one of these horrible crimes, the Algorithm always forgave.

Always gave him another chance.

Always remedied his mistakes.

And it did so in a way that ensured Hugo's young, innocent, naive little brain would understand the horrible, disgusting, painful, tragic, and highly illegal act that was taking place. It delivered this lesson to him by sending a piercing sound through the air whenever one of these actions occurred, and the noise could only be stopped once the error had been rectified.

At first, the Algorithm showed him the solution—moving him in view of the camera or returning the device to his left ear—instantly stopping the piercing sound that always sent him into a fit of tears.

The time it took for the mechanical arm to spring into action continued to increase until finally came the day when Hugo realized the correlation between the sound and his actions and no longer needed the mechanical arm.

Until never again did Hugo perform one of these heinous crimes against the Algorithm.

Or any other crime, for that matter.

3.

THE ALGORITHM WAS ALWAYS GROWING—in 1s and in 0s and in a wealth of knowledge about love and the American people and what a perfect world was meant to look like and how it could be achieved. It was exponentially expanding, in all directions, toward all infinites, pulling America into a bigger and brighter and more perfect future. Even as the nation slept, as the people rested, as their minds shut down for the night, the Algorithm was still running simulations, a nearly incalculable amount, which considered every possible and hardly probable path the nation could travel the following day. It saw the future of every American person, all their potential futures, in every imaginable combination. Then, after carefully assessing each of those futures in an individual and collective capacity, the Algorithm created the singular path most advantageous to America as a whole.

Then spent the day nudging the entirety of America down their individually assigned routes, which, in their totality, led America to its perfect day.

It was a complicated science involving even more complicated mathematics, both of which required an advanced understanding of incredibly sophisticated systems regarding infinities and the multilayers of reality. But the Algorithm was the most intellectually advanced entity on the planet, likely the most sophisticated creation in this ever-expanding universe, and so, to the Algorithm, these otherwise impossible performances were just something it did to occupy its time while the human beings it watched over slept for the night.

But discovering the optimal path for America's tomorrow was not the only thing the Algorithm did while America rested for the night. It also ran entire factories, controlled whole warehouses, and oversaw thousands of studios scattered across the nation, inside which billions of machines prepared for their perfect tomorrow. Meals were prepped, drinks were formulated, the cars that traveled the tunnels below were repaired and recharged, clothing was stitched, billboards were designed, scripts were written, shows were edited, and perfect days not yet had were created in their entirety, until all that was needed was for the human beings assigned to those particular events to wake up and pick up their phones and follow the steps perfectly assigned to them.

And as if all of that was still somehow not enough, the Algorithm kept working, kept calculating, kept evaluating, kept gathering. It redesigned restaurants, re-furnished complexes, cleaned entire cities, repainted every fence, mowed every blade of grass. And then, as the sun began to rise, hidden behind the American Northern Lights, the doors of those warehouses and factories opened and drones flooded the sky with packages in claws, cars took to the tunnels, airplanes rolled to their proper terminal, machines of various usages reported to duty, and the alarm began to ring gently in Hugo's left ear, growing louder and more intense until the Data Gathering Device detected that he was fully awake.

The first thing Hugo did each morning was grab his phone to perform his morning scroll.

He answered a series of questions to better help the Algorithm understand his quality of sleep and the visuals of his dreams. He then scrolled through dozens of Data Gathering Profiles curated for him by the Algorithm. Some profiles were of his neighbors, others were of kids from around town and across the nation, while others were of his favorite celebrities.

It was on these profiles that the Algorithm curated a person's existence for the viewing pleasures of another: pictures from that user's life, videos from their many adventures, and reviews given to them by those who had gathered data with them in the past. It neatly organized onto a single page who the person was, what they believed, and what they represented—their interests and their disinterests, where their views landed on this topic and the other, how much they had changed throughout their life and what changes they were projected to undergo in the future.

And as a person gathered more data, the more the information on their Data Gathering Profiles accumulated, grew, matured—made for a clearer picture of who they were, who they had been, and who they were likely to become.

As was the case for everything in America, these Data Gathering Profiles were personalized for the one viewing them, ensuring the viewer saw only the information most relevant to them. The information Hugo saw on Lamar T. Haddington's Data Gathering Profile was not the same as what his neighbor saw. What his mother saw on his own profile differed from what his father saw.

And so on.

After Hugo reached the end of the profiles assigned to him on any given morning, a new application would automatically open on his phone, one that the Algorithmic Corporation had created as a way of teaching young children to stay connected with the happenings around the nation and the world and their local city. The articles featured on this application were written in a language that was easy for a kid of Hugo's age to understand. They were short, and photographs were always featured, along with animated videos.

Last of all, he was shown his schedule for the day, all of the events planned on his behalf by the Algorithm to ensure that not only the nation had a perfect day, but that he too had a perfect day.

* * *

At the age of four, as Hugo performed yet another morning scroll, he saw the event on his daily schedule that he had waited his entire life for, all four years.

At the sight of this event, he jumped out of bed and ran down the hall, toward his parents' bedroom, yelling:

"Mommy! Daddy! Mommy! Daddy! I'm going to school! I'm going to school!"

When he reached their room, he found his parents sitting in bed with their phones in their hands.

"Our little Hugo's going to school," his mother said, jumping out of bed to hug her son.

"And look at these projections," said his father in reference to the charts he had open on his phone—bar graphs and pie charts and scatter plots created to portray the predictions of his son's successes in school.

"Our little boy is going to be so smart one day," said his mother, kissing little Hugo on his cheek.

"And he's going to be quite the little Patriot," said his father, who then jumped out of bed and ran toward Hugo and lifted him up and twirled him over his head, round and round and round again.

"We are so proud of you and everything you are going to do," said his mother.

"So very proud, indeed," said his father, as he continued twirling Hugo over his head.

Hugo was given an unusually large meal for breakfast that day, ensuring he had the energy he needed for his first day of school. His plate had on it five pancakes stacked high, smothered in melted butter and syrup and a small scoop of peanut butter, along with a pile of berries, some scrambled eggs, two strips of bacon, three links of sausage, some corned beef hash, and smoked salmon atop a toasted everything bagel. And to help him wash it all down, he was given an extra-large cup of chocolate milk—the sort of cup that was so large he needed two hands to drink it.

As he ate his enormous meal, his parents went on endlessly about their excitement for their son's first day of school.

"If I had grown up in the time you get to grow up in," said his mother, "my head wouldn't be filled with so much unimportant information, most of which is just an outright lie."

And his father said, "If I had grown up today, I would be a heck of a lot smarter than I am now, that's for sure."

They reminded him that his teachers were employees of the Algorithmic Corporation and were there to enforce the rules of the Algorithm and to serve their nation. They reminded him that the Algorithm had already determined that everything he was going to be taught inside his private pod would be very important for his future, so he needed to listen and obey. They reminded him that all of the time he spent on the playground was to be taken incredibly seriously for it was an opportunity to gather data that could help to make his world even more perfect. They reminded him that every person he saw at school would have the chance to write a review about him and that all of America would be able to see that review—including the Algorithm, the President, and his future perfect match.

Therefore, it was essential to be kind to all people and to always be smiling.

Always, always, always.

Hugo nodded along with his parents' reminders, his mouth constantly chewing.

At one moment, as his parents continued to talk and he continued to eat, a three-foot-tall robot called the House Maid-9000 rolled up to his side with socks and shoes in hand. Hugo stuck out his feet as the House Maid-9000 slid on his socks and tied his shoes tightly. Then it brushed the crumbs off his shirt, cleaned the stains off his pants, rubbed the syrup off his cheeks, and fixed the little strands of hair that had been messed up during the frenzy of breakfast.

Before rolling away, the House Maid-9000 handed Hugo and his parents their daily pills and glasses of water to help them drink them down.

Then:

The elevator dinged, indicating that the cars were approaching their spots below their home. The three of them—father, mother, and son—entered the elevator and rode it down to the tunnels below. Hugo had a brand-new backpack. His father had his satchel. His mother held a tote.

The elevator doors opened just as the three cars parked.

Hugo's mother got into the first, his father in the second, and Hugo in the third—then off they went, zip-zappin' through the underground tunnels of San Antonio to their individual destinations.

As the car took Hugo to school, the television screen where the windshield used to be played for him his favorite show.

"Have you ever wondered what inspired Lamar T. Haddington to save America from the imperfect madhouse it once was? Today, we have your answer."

Made in the USA
Las Vegas, NV
05 October 2024

96332649R00121